One Life

Out of the Shadow of a Family Secret

One Life

Out of the Shadow of a Family Secret

Margaret Sugden

LeMar Publications

Published by LeMar Publications 2009
7 Queensgate, Beverley. HU17 8NN

All rights reserved. No part of this publication may be reproduced, stored in a retrieval system, or transmitted, in any form or by any means, without the prior permission in writing of LeMar Publications, or as expressly permitted by law, or under terms agreed with the appropriate reprographics rights organisation. Enquiries concerning reproduction outside the scope of the above should be sent to LeMar Publications at the address above.

ISBN 978-0-9561721-0-5

The moral right of Margaret Sugden to be identified as the author of this work has been asserted in accordance with the Copyright Designs and Patents Act 1988.

Design by Andrew Jackson
Printed and bound by Central Print Services
University of Hull

Dedication

In memory of my late husband Peter; for Paul, Andrew, Jeanine and Darren; my grandchildren; Toby, John, Michael, Rebecca, Adam and Christopher, and my friends Ruth and Stan, Christine and Bill, as well as Michael, Fenella and Philip, all of whom enriched my life beyond measure.

Acknowledgements

My thanks to Peter Didsbury, my tutor at the University of Hull, for his stalwart attempts at teaching me English grammar and for believing in and encouraging me. Also Robin Saltonstall in recognition of his encouragement and support as well as editing early drafts of this book, and last but not least to Andrew Jackson for rescuing my old photographs and bringing them new life to enhance the illustration and design of this book.

Contents

Introduction

CHAPTER ONE
    A Child of Wartime   1

CHAPTER TWO
    Returning Home   11

CHAPTER THREE
    Growing Up   21

CHAPTER FOUR
    A Shocking Revelation   33

CHAPTER FIVE
    Leaving Home   41

CHAPTER SIX
    My Day in Juvenile Court   57

CHAPTER SEVEN
    Life in the Women's Royal Air Force, 1953   69

CHAPTER EIGHT
    Mount Batten   79

CHAPTER NINE
    St Eval   95

CHAPTER TEN
    Uxbridge   111

CHAPTER ELEVEN
    Blackpool 1955   123

CHAPTER TWELVE
    My Stay in Bradford   137

CHAPTER THIRTEEN
    A Posting to Malta   149

CHAPTER FOURTEEN
    Blackpool RAF Transit Camp   159

CHAPTER FIFTEEN
    RAF North Weald – A Life Crisis   165

CHAPTER SIXTEEN
    High Wycombe Bentley Priory   185

CHAPTER SEVENTEEN
    Bahrain 1965   193

CHAPTER EIGHTEEN
    Naphill 1967: A New Baby and Betrayal   213

CHAPTER NINETEEN
    Singapore 1968   229

CHAPTER TWENTY
    RAF Halton: The Last Posting   251

Introduction

This is the book I always said that I would write one day. Many years ago, when I was in my late twenties, a friend suggested I write about my childhood days and the family secret, but, at that time, I was far too busy simply getting on with living my life.

Now however, many, many years have passed and I have lots more exciting events to relate. Now I have the time both to look back and to still live in the present.

Our past affects who we are in a multitude of different ways but I firmly believe that we are all responsible for our own actions and that blaming the past only delays our own progress and cognitive development. Accepting this responsibility for ourselves allows us to take charge of our lives.

Friends are so important. We cannot choose our relatives but we can choose our friends. Mine have enriched my life and I could not have written this book without them. They are so much a part of it and it was they who taught me just what love, loyalty, and nurturing is all about.

Kindness and caring in one's professional working life brings more for the recipient than for the employer: or does it? Contentment in a job done to the best of my ability is invaluable to me. Conversely not being perfect, sometimes making mistakes, and getting things wrong is fundamental to our lives as human beings and makes one far more comfortable to be with!

I am neither famous nor remarkable. I have told my story just as it happened and leave any judgements and conclusions to you, my readers.

Thank you so much for taking the trouble to read it.

Margaret Sugden
February 2009

Although this book recalls truthfully the events in my life, a few of the names have been changed where this might otherwise have caused someone distress or embarrassment.

Chapter One

A Child of Wartime

The earliest memory I have of my childhood is of being evacuated to Reading where I was put with a family who were not happy to have me. Their son was at war and they had no other children, but they did have a spare room, and so they were obliged to take in an evacuee. There was no check in those days on the people taking an evacuee, or indeed, whether they were suitable to care for a child at all. I was going to be at the mercy of this family and I was apprehensive and afraid. They, I'm sure, felt less than pleased at having a child who they'd assumed to have come from the slums of London. I was given my meals on my own, in the kitchen, and treated as an outsider. I was then just six years old and felt alone in this world.

These people did not seem to want me or like me. Fortunately, for me, this only lasted a very short time. News soon arrived that their son had been wounded and was on his way home and so, I found myself on my way to Paddington Station with an address label pinned to my coat, and my gas mask slung round my neck. I was being sent back home like an unwanted parcel. For the life of me I could not place whatever or wherever 'home' was. I had been put on to the train, unceremoniously, without any instructions.

I remember sitting, staring out into the darkness beyond the window, and listening to the sounds the train made. First of all, there was a hiss of steam, followed by the whistle as we started off, and then a slow chuff, chuff, chuff which gradually got faster.

One Life

Chagatai chug, tickety boo – Chagatai chug, tickety boo it went. As I listened I was reassured and it lulled me to sleep.

When I awoke it was to hustle and bustle all around me. We had reached Paddington Station. People were getting cases down, and putting their coats on. I looked out from the train but could see very little due to the blackout. Feeling more than a little afraid I followed the other passengers and peered down at the gap between the train and the platform; it seemed a long way off. Then I felt strong arms lift me from behind and across the gap. Looking round I found a man's face peering into mine. Suddenly I heard a loud droning, followed by a swishing sound, and then a shuddering crump. For a split second, everyone was very still and then pandemonium broke out. The man's mouth was moving but I could hear nothing of what he was saying in the din. He swept me up and now everyone was running.

There were more whooshes and crumps as the man took me to the stationmaster's office and handed me over. He explained that he had found me struggling to reach the platform from the carriage and that there appeared to be no-one with me. They both looked at me, noticing the address label on my coat. Then the man said he had to go, and left me in the stationmaster's care.

I felt safe with this big kindly man in uniform who was assuring me that he would find my mum and dad for me though it took some time to locate my mum. She was not at the home address on the label as she was working in the munitions factory and had not received the telegram telling her that I was being sent home. I do not remember anything about my mum at this stage in my life. I had spent very little time with her. She was furious about the way that I'd just been labelled and dumped on a train, and said so in very colourful language to the stationmaster when she arrived to pick me up.

A Child of Wartime

During the short period I had been in Reading, my mother had been bombed out of her flat in the Fulham Road. One morning, on arriving home after a night shift at the munitions factory, she'd found that her block of flats had been destroyed. Her front door had been blown in and a great lump of her bedroom ceiling had somehow got itself neatly under the counterpane on her dust covered, but otherwise undisturbed, bed. Everything else was reduced to rubble. Only a few weeks before this my father had died of tuberculosis. I never knew him or even that he had died. I can't remember anything prior to being evacuated to Reading.

Having been bombed out, my mother had moved to Tooting Broadway in the suburbs of London which was, conveniently, on the underground route. When she finally arrived to collect me she appeared angry and impatient. She had a thin, drawn look about her and her raven-black hair was swept up at the front and sides with the rest of it hidden by a head scarf tied on the top of her head. There was a muscle twitching in her right cheek and I was soon to recognise this as a sign of her temper rising. There was no welcoming hug; instead, and irritably, she just told me to hurry up. She didn't seem to want me around anymore than the people in Reading had.

Arriving at the tube station I found myself propelled along in a sea of bodies and, finding myself at the top of a moving staircase, I froze in horror. She tugged at my arm and then pushed me on to what looked like moving metal teeth. Wobbling desperately, I grabbed first her coat, and then her legs, and hung on for dear life. Soon, with me still shaking violently, we were at the bottom and the metal teeth were disappearing before my eyes. Pushed forward, and yanked up by my arm, I flew over those teeth to safety and, propelled forward once again by the sheer mass of people around us. We finally came to rest on to the

One Life

platform for Tooting Broadway.

There, to one side, was the big, dark mouth of a huge tunnel and I felt its stuffy warm breath and heard a strange rocking and shushing sound. Suddenly a train swooped like an enormous red bat into the station. The doors swished open and the tight-packed bodies around us shoved us forward and onto the train. I held on tight to my mother's hand, trying to look up at her for reassurance. I couldn't see her face but only the sea of legs and knees that was packed in so close around me that I could hardly breathe.

I stood cringing and waiting for this swaying nightmare to end. When I did manage a look at my mother she looked so cross and forbidding that it stopped me from shuffling closer when we managed to gain a seat on reaching the last few stops. Now stations were flashing by and I saw glimpses of their lights, their colourful advertisements, and the crowds of people that were packed onto their platforms. Then our carriage rocked fiercely from side to side as the train rushed on.

At last we arrived at our station. Here there were people sleeping on the floor under blankets. In places we had to step over them before ascending another of those awful moving staircases and on, out into the inky darkness of the blackout. All houses had to have heavy curtains, and the street lighting was turned off so that the German planes could not see where to drop their bombs. We got on a bus that took us the three stops, that before had seemed to be a long walk in the pitch black, to reach our flat on Heaton Road. I was so exhausted I fell asleep whilst my mother made a drink. She woke me and I climbed into a big double bed and fell into a deep sleep.

Mum had taken in a lodger, something which was expected if you had a spare room, and therefore I had to sleep with her as we

A Child of Wartime

only had two bedrooms. I did not like sleeping with her; being a bit of a fidget I was often told to lie still or I'd be put under the bed on the cold lino.

During the ensuing months I found myself left very much to my own devices – a latch key kid. I kept the key around my neck and let myself into the house after school. As my mum was so often out I soon learned to become responsible and not lose the key. If I did I would spend many cold and miserable hours waiting for her to come back and I'd be punished for losing it into the bargain.

I walked along the common to Goringe Park School. There were a couple of air-raid bunkers on the common, mounds of grass hiding them from view. These were spread far apart. I never remember being near enough to run to one when an air-raid started. Instead we had been told to run to the nearest house and ask to be taken into their shelter.

One day my friend Monica and I were dawdling home from school. We hadn't heard a siren but did hear the droning of aircraft engines, and the well-known sounds of swishes and crumps, could suddenly be heard from not far away. A plane appeared over our heads. It was so low that we could see the pilot in the cockpit. We fled in terror, shrapnel flying around us as we ran. Having dropped his bombs he was strafing us with cannon and machine gun fire. Mum had said that we lived on the bombers' route back out over the coast and that they dumped anything they had left before running the gauntlet of our coastal guns. I'd lost my shoe whilst running and didn't dare to stop and pick it up. Reaching the nearest house, out of breath and panting, we knocked frantically on the door, shouting, 'Let us in, please let us in!' Getting no answer we crouched in the doorway, terrified, but at the same time agog with excitement at what we'd just seen.

One Life

We waited for the distant sound of the plane to fade. Then, very carefully we peeked out from the doorway, fearful that another plane might be coming. Eventually we resumed our walk home carefully. The all-clear had sounded but we dared not trust anything at that moment. We had just had a close encounter with death, not game-playing death, but the real thing. I looked for my shoe. There it was, a piece of shrapnel embedded in it. We stared in awe. 'Coo!' I said, and shuddered: 'I could have been in that shoe!' I kept that piece of shrapnel for years.

We certainly had a story to tell all our mates, and there was plenty of time to do it. School consisted mostly of time spent in the shelters. The bombing raids were a constant feature of life at that time.

For many nights now the constant bombing had been terrible. The lodger and I would dive for cover under the dining room table as bombs dropped all around us. My mum said, 'If your time's up, it's up. So why bother?' Mr and Mrs Savage downstairs had a Morrison Shelter in their front room and we could join them, together with their fox terrier Fourpence, if a raid started. But my mother said, 'There's no way I'm sharing a shelter with no bloody dog!' So she'd stay upstairs in bed.

Walking to school one morning we found what looked like the remains of an aircraft that had crashed into our school. I was mesmerised; was this a real 'Jerry' plane? Could it be the one that had nearly got us? Where was the pilot? Later, a kid in our school boasted that it was his garden the pilot had landed in and his mum had taken a pitchfork to him. The police who'd collected him had said that the kid's mum had been really brave.

Then our school was bombed and we all had to go to another one nearby – again spending most of our time in the shelters. To keep our spirits up we recited our multiplication tables and told

A Child of Wartime

each other stories. As a result we had very little real schooling throughout the war and this was to cause me a lot of difficulties in the years ahead.

The coming of the doodle-bug was an awful shock. I can vividly remember the sound of the engine, the whining, and then the sudden quiet as the engine stopped. I'd hold my breath and pray that it didn't land on us. Then there'd be the crump sound from some way off and the huge relief that I was still alive and uninjured. After one really bad night we came back upstairs from the shelter to find a hole in the ceiling of our kitchen. A large piece of plaster was moving on the kitchen floor! It turned out that our cat was underneath it. Fortunately, he was unhurt except for his pride. Our chimney-pot had been blown straight through the ceiling.

That morning was to be very upsetting for me. I found out that my best friend Monica, a petite girl with long brown hair, dark brown eyes, and a very cheeky grin, had been killed along with all her family. They'd all lived just across the road from us. The blast from a bomb had zigzagged across two streets, demolishing the two houses opposite and our chimney-pot. Blast from bombs behaved in very erratic ways.

As we had done on so many other occasions, we sang the hymn *Through the night of doubt and sorrow* at school assembly that morning – only this time it was for my best friend. I cried and cried. I could not understand why this had to happen to Monica. Mum said, 'Don't be so stupid, she's probably a lot better out of it.' But it didn't help. I only cried more and got smacked for whinging. I was glad when I could go to bed and I cried myself to sleep that night. I didn't make a really close friend again for some time and walking to school became a solitary affair. I often played in the bombed-out places in our

One Life

street but never in the remains of Monica's house. It was the first thing I saw on leaving my house every morning. This was what 'being at war' really meant.

My Aunt Winnie was tall and thickset with long blond hair. She had a very domineering nature, especially towards Jimmy, her mild mannered Jewish husband who adored her. He was a short, wizened man who always appeared to be bending over. Perhaps this was because he was a tailor. The rag trade was flourishing in London at this time. He had thinning hair on top and eyes that appeared to be taking everything in.

Winnie and Jimmy, who lived in Chelsea, had decided to come and stop at our flat for a couple of nights, saying, 'We're coming to you to get a night's sleep. The bombing is so bad we haven't had a full night's sleep for ages.'

My mum said, 'Fat chance of that! It's even worse here. The Jerries dump any bombs they've got left on us.'

But Winnie and Jimmy did not believe it could be worse.

That night it was as bad as usual and, on getting up, we found them both packed and waiting for the early bus. Jimmy had a black eye and Winnie said she was a 'bag of nerves'. It turned out that during the night Jimmy had opened the door leading down to the garden, instead of the toilet door and, stepping out into space, had landed face down in the sand bucket which we kept ready to put fires out. That was his story anyway. He'd got a real shiner to his right eye. Whatever the truth was they couldn't wait to get home.

Soon after this I was evacuated for a second time. This time I was taken to Arnold, a village in Nottingham, to stay with an old spinster. She had no relatives and had never had children in the house.

Aunt Emma, as I was told to call her, was tall with long

A Child of Wartime

greying hair which she kept in a bun at the back of her head. She had an aristocratic air about her but I rarely saw her without her apron on. She was also a staunch chapel-goer, and proved to be kind and caring. Her life consisted of daily routines that rarely changed: chapel on Sunday mornings was a must. We'd set off across the fields, meeting up with the other people that my aunt knew. I attended Sunday school whilst the adults had their service and we'd join them in the main church just before the end.

I learnt most of the 'thou shalts' and 'thou shalt nots' and listened to the Bible stories. These teachings left a lasting impression on me and I enjoyed the atmosphere and friendship that prevailed. I was to experience several different religions in the future years ahead and these would give me a broader outlook on my own faith.

After lunch Aunt Emma would nod off in the chair by the fire for a couple of hours and I'd have to sit quietly in a chair whilst she dozed. It was to prove an invaluable lesson for me, not only in self-control, but also in using quiet periods of time to escape into the world of my own imagination. On the whole, my time spent with Aunt Emma was very happy.

I remember going out to play in the huge green fields with stiles to climb over. I loved crossing the pastures full of cows that looked you in the eye. Once I mistook a bull for a cow, and after staring at it face-to-face for a while, I suddenly felt an urgent need to run and ended up flying over a fence – tearing my knickers in the process.

I also remember the little things, like being given a clean hanky to put in my pocket for school each day. On my ninth birthday Aunt Emma bought me a bicycle! And for Christmas she gave me a miniature carved double bed, with satin covers and a bolster, and two dolls, one white and one black, whilst on

One Life

another birthday she bought me a small doll's pram that was my pride and joy. These were to be my only childhood presents of note. Sometimes she'd tell me off but it was always done fairly and kindly.

Aunt Emma's house was detached with a fairly large garden at the back in which she'd had a swing made which was suspended from a tree for me. The garden led into her comfortable kitchen which was the most used room in the house. I remember the lovely cooking smells that welcomed me home from school.

Sometimes I'd bunk off from school with a friend and we'd wander off into the fields where we'd sit making daisy chains, and daydreaming. On other occasions we'd scrump apples from orchards and thoroughly enjoyed our stolen booty!

On the whole I remember this as a very happy period in my life and it was to have a profound effect in helping me cope when, with the war almost over, I finally returned to my mother's home.

Chapter Two
Returning Home

I returned home just before the war ended to find that the neighbours had developed a real camaraderie. Almost everyone had lost something or someone, and helping each other out had become the normal thing to do. Not my mother though – she didn't associate with the neighbours.

I soon settled down with new friends, playing hopscotch in the street and larking in the bombed out houses. These places had been made no-go areas to us and this made playing in them all the more exiting. There were gaping holes, where floors should be, and rickety staircases. We rummaged around finding old pieces of mirror, broken beds and all sorts of other bits and pieces to play with and we'd shin up or down ropes which we'd hung from the beams. Our imagination knew no bounds and included war games – with spies and 'Jerries' to flush out and capture. Like my friends, I did not think of the danger these bombed houses represented. Then Mum told me I was not to play out in the street when I got home from school. I was to stay in and get my jobs done.

My mother was out for long periods and I soon became bored with staying indoors. Whenever any friends called I was 'off out to play', forgetting the meal I was supposed to be cooking. One special memory I have is of the celebrations for VE day and the street parties. All the neighbours clubbed together and prepared food, arranging, setting up, and laying out trestle tables down the middle of the street. My mother was never around at these times.

One Life

I was nonetheless included in the parties, together with all the other children from the street.

My mother, who had become a widow in her mid twenties, was now in her thirties. Her husband, George, my father, was French by birth. I overheard her telling someone else that he had been in his final year internship to become a doctor when he contracted tuberculosis. He died whilst I was an evacuee in Reading. He had been the love of her life. There was a small photograph of him on the mantelpiece. In this photograph he was tall with blond wavy hair, and I thought he looked very distinguished. I used to look at him and tell him that I wanted to be a nurse or a doctor too.

This is the only photograph of me with my mother. I was about 3. At the time, she was married to George LeCorney, who probably took the picture. This appears to have been a happy period of her life. Unfortunately, George only had another 2 years or so to live.

My mother was small and slim and not unattractive when in a good mood. Unfortunately her good moods were few. She worked in the rag trade in London during the years following the war and developed a good dress sense. Most of the rag trade

Returning Home

belonged to hard-working Jewish refugees from the holocaust in London at that time. My mother often boasted about how she had got the first job she had applied for after the war – as a seamstress in London.

On arriving to apply for a job it was a novel experience for her to be faced with the complex over-locking machines with their bobbins and complicated threading systems. Undaunted, she lied and said, 'Of course I'm experienced in using them,' and she quickly developed the skills needed.

She worked in the rag trade for some time, learning sewing, cutting out, basting, and all the other skills necessary to good dressmaker. She also did domestic work for a couple of middle class families in London. Gradually she developed her own sewing business and circle of customers and these included the parents of debutantes who were still presented at court and 'came out' in London.

My mother was also skilled at making Christmas and wedding cakes, and decorated them beautifully ready for sale. She developed this sideline despite the rationing which still existed. It never appeared to bother her. She managed to get black market eggs and butter quite easily from her contacts. She'd a capacity to work very long, hard hours at both her sewing and her cake making. I had to do the washing up, the housework, and have meals ready when she came in from work. She was extremely house-proud and I got many a thrashing when she said something was not up to the standard she required.

I never saw her without a cigarette. When sewing, the cigarette often hung from her mouth and she had nicotine stained fingers and nails. She became even more bad tempered when there were no cigarettes to hand. I remember vividly being sent out to buy her cigarettes. I dared not go back until I had managed

13

One Life

to get them and this meant standing outside the public house door and pleading with an adult to 'get me a packet of fags for me mum'. I hated having to do this, but I was still more terrified to go back without the cigarettes. I vowed I'd never let cigarettes control my life.

Not surprisingly Mum's very violent temper, and her uncanny knack for causing a scene with family members, often led to her being left out of family events. My friends were also very wary. One morning my friend Sylvia called for me and just missed getting hit by a tin of beans whizzing past me as I ran down the stairs to escape one of my mother's tantrums. After that I called for Sylvia and spent a good deal of time at her house.

Once we were playing at dressing up in my mother's bedroom when I suddenly heard the sound of a key turning in the front door. Panic stricken, I shoved Sylvia into the wardrobe, locked her in to keep the door shut, and I rushed into the kitchen offering to make Mum a cup of tea. She said she didn't feel too good and so would go to bed. Somehow I had to get Sylvia from the wardrobe, down the stairs and out of the house. I suggested to my mother that I fill a hot water bottle for her, and then, dashing back, I let a shaking Sylvia out of the wardrobe whispering to her to sneak out quietly whilst I kept my mother occupied. Fortunately we did not get caught on this occasion!

Sylvia was now my closest friend. Her mum was a tubby, motherly, loving person and was always kind and caring towards me. Sylvia's Nan also lived with them. She could be a caustic, cantankerous old woman but I clicked with her from the beginning. I was later to have the privilege of being with her during her last illness. Sylvia remained my closest friend for some years.

One thing that stands out most in my mind about this period is

Returning Home

getting out of bed at 6 o'clock on cold mornings and seeing those amazing fern like patterns that the icy frosts made on the inside of the windows. I would put on my dressing gown, shivering from cold, go into the kitchen and put the kettle on. I'd then switch on the small single bar electric fire in the corner of the kitchen ready for my mother and me to have breakfast. If I over slept I knew I would be in for it. My mother would slam doors and bang things about. Sometimes she would throw things at my head whilst I was lying in bed, like my shoes if I had forgotten to put them away properly the evening before.

I hated doing those cold early morning jobs when it was still dark outside, but I had to do them before going to school. They included cleaning the front door step with a pumice stone, shining the knocker with Brasso – with freezing cold fingers, and clearing out the ashes from the fire grate and setting it ready with 'paper bombs'. These had to be made out of rolled up pieces of newspaper tied into a loose knot and placed under the pieces of coal to help in getting the fire going. One of the worst jobs was filling the coal-scuttle ready for the evening from that horrible coal-hole in the kitchen where spiders and mice lurked. I also had jobs to do in the evening before my mother and the lodger got home from work. Sometimes I would forget to do a job, and then I would get punished. Usually this consisted of a good clout around the head, if I didn't dodge quickly enough, and then I'd be sent to bed without any tea.

I remember once putting the vegetables on for dinner and then going out to play and the burnt potatoes that resulted from me forgetting them. Don, the lodger, would often stick up for me at such times. It was quite usual for me to be locked in my room as a punishment and then my mother would go out. Don would unlock the door, let me out for a while, and then lock me in again

One Life

before my mother returned. Eventually he left and my mother put me into the small box room the lodger vacated. I was thrilled to have a room and bed to myself.

I now attended Links Road School. The war was over and I had to sit the eleven plus exam. I had missed a good deal of schooling during the war years and, though this had not concerned me at the time, I now found that I could not understand the questions on the paper as I could hardly read. Formerly I'd thoroughly enjoyed school, seeing it as a place to have fun. I'd played the teachers up and deliberately taken the blame for other pupil's misdeeds, enjoying the attention I received. I remember sitting outside the Headmistress's office learning 'The Lady of Shallot'. There were a number of verses but I'd enjoyed reciting them.

I knitted a jumper for myself, during class, with a complicated lace pattern; this can just be seen in my school photo. I also made a blouse. I could sew well from having had to do it for my mother. Of necessity I'd become proficient at sewing hems, blind stitching, finishing off, tacking and pressing and in folding the finished garments ready to be delivered to the clients. I did not enjoy ironing, or sewing at home: it had to be perfect and I got it wrong on many occasions, but making a blouse at school, cutting it out myself and using the sewing machine, was different. My teacher was delighted with the finished garment and took me to the headmistress to show her. This was something new to me and it

Returning Home

was a wonderful feeling to be praised and encouraged for my efforts. I had taught myself to use my mother's sewing machine when she was out. The treadle was quite heavy to use. I had to be very careful to see that I left it as my mother had so that she would not find me out.

I hated cleaning up after sewing at home – picking up all those pins and trying to sweep away all the bits of cotton clinging to the carpet. Bits of cotton would walk everywhere, even down the stairs. We didn't have hoovers in those days. Sunday dinner washing up was another job I hated, and oven cleaning day, when the oven had to be taken apart and cleaned from top to bottom, was a complete nightmare. It took ages, often most of the afternoon.

I joined the local church just around the corner, and then the choir, as a soprano, gaining a medal for choral singing. The vicar tried to get me to be confirmed. I took the lessons but refused as I felt I was not ready to take the vows and was not good enough to live up to them. Although it was expected that a member of the choir would be confirmed, he understood my reasoning and allowed me to stay.

I joined the Guides and the St John Ambulance too. Along with the church, I thoroughly enjoyed all three organisations. I collected badges in the guides, gained confidence in myself, and became a patrol leader. Joining the St John Ambulance fulfilled part of my ambition to become a nurse. Choosing which uniform to wear on St George's Day might have proved a dilemma, but being in the choir relieved me of that responsibility.

In the end, however, these hobbies only turned out to be another way in which my mother could punish me for not doing my jobs properly – she'd simply stop me attending them. If an exam was coming up, or a special evening event, I learned to

One Life

keep it from her. If she found that I had a special reason for going anywhere she'd stop me. I lived in fear of her finding out. I tried so hard to please her. I determined to do my jobs especially well, only to find I had not made a bed, or polished the floor in the bedroom to her satisfaction.

I soon realised that how the floor actually looked was irrelevant. On one occasion I had, as usual, made her bed with envelope corners, polished the floor until it was gleaming, and made sure there was no fluff under the bed. I'd even put the finishing touches to it all by laying her brush set on her dressing table neatly. I then went and told her I had finished her bedroom. She came and, before she'd even really looked at it, she said, 'Do it again, it's not clean, there is dust everywhere.'

I looked and looked but could see no dust. Feeling very angry and sulky I stood at the bedroom window watching the children playing in the back gardens. I hated Mum at that moment and wished I could be with them playing. Then I sat down on the floor and, taking a piece of string out of my pocket, played cats cradles, telling myself I didn't care if she hit me. I would run away to Aunt Emma's. I waited for a while and then I went to her and told her that I had done it again. She looked around and said, 'There you are – why couldn't you do it properly in the first place?'

After this episode I never re-did a job again. Instead I'd hide comics in the wardrobe under the newspaper placed at the bottom for shoes to be put on. I was allowed one comic a week: 'Laurel and Hardy', which I really enjoyed. I would sometimes just sit on the floor with a duster in my hand imagining that I was a famous dancer or a fairy and could just fly away.

I learned many survival techniques. When Mum locked me in my room and went out just leaving me there, I'd take the

Returning Home

newspaper from the bottom of the wardrobe and, sliding it under the door, I'd push the key out with a hair clip from my side so that the key would drop onto the newspaper. Then I'd carefully pull the newspaper back under the door to my side, pick the key up from it and unlock the door. I could then go down into the kitchen, cut round the butter and cheese evenly, and make myself a sandwich. I would then lock myself back in from my side of the door and, putting the key on the floor I would hit it with the end of a wooden coat hanger so that it was knocked back under the door. I did this so that when my mother found the key on the floor I could say it was there because the phone had rung and I'd shaken the door trying to get out to answer it.

My mother had two men friends that were always around. One was called Mr Nicholson. I thought of him as 'Old Nick' since he appeared very elderly to me. He was distinguished looking. He had white hair, and was always smartly dressed. He used a cane with a silver top to it and he had an artificial leg. I believe he'd lost his leg in the war. He was always nice and friendly and often took my side when my mother shouted at me. He took my mother to shows in London and on rare occasions he'd suggest that Mum let me go as well. He also owned a skiff moored on the Thames. I was taken with them on one holiday for two weeks. A canvas cover was erected over the boat for them and a small tent was erected on the bank for me. I enjoyed this holiday.

Usually Mum would leave me to care for myself when she went away. I remember her going off with Nick soon after the war and leaving me to look after the lodger. This happened a few times before the lodger finally left to go back home. During the war these lodgers, who had worked in the factories away from their homes helping with the war effort, had had to be taken in if

One Life

you had an empty room. Although Mum could have asked our lodger to leave, she did not do so. The money for his board and lodging was far too useful.

On the whole I did not particularly like or dislike 'Old Nick'; he was just part of our life. I knew he was married as I heard Mum talking about his wife to her sister Winnie. It appeared that Nick and his wife both led their own lives and she knew about my mother. Mum treated me better in his company because he'd stick up for me and she always seemed more relaxed and happy when he was around. He never made me feel that I was in the way, which was more than I can say for Edward – her other long standing male friend. Edward was a bit of a creep. He was unmarried, of medium build with dark greasy slicked back hair. I just didn't like him, and the feeling was mutual. My mother usually took the key from around my neck and sent me out until a certain time if they were staying in. He was always pussyfooting around my mother. I heard my mother tell Winnie that he was boring and only came for a good meal. They sometimes went out together and had the odd weekend away. I don't know why she kept seeing him but she did. He was always there in the background, popping up, and he kept on calling on my mother every so often throughout these post war years.

Chapter Three

Growing Up

The years growing up in the London suburb of Mitcham were eventful years for me. Although there were many household jobs for me to do, I was often left to my own devices. With my mounting list of hobbies there was never much time left to be lonely. Sylvia remained my closest friend but I had made some others too.

Doris was one. She lived just across the road and to the right of the gap where Monica's house use to be. This space was now put to good use on Bonfire Nights, but no one mentioned the past on these occasions.

Doris was a tall girl for her age with blond hair. She was good-natured, like her mum who was a plump round happy go lucky person who had time for anyone, and loved a good gossip. She was not unkind but she was outspoken if she felt it was warranted. Doris's mum often took me in when I was locked out on a cold rainy day and not able to go in until a certain time. My mother was always ready to give me money to go to the pictures. However I had often seen the pictures when on picture duty with St John Ambulance, so I'd save this money for my Guides' or St John's activities, just in case my mother wouldn't give me any.

On one occasion Mum flew into a temper when I had not done the housework to her satisfaction, and locked me in my room. She was going out to see a show and planned to stay in a hotel overnight with 'Old Nick'.

'You can wait until I come back tomorrow to be let out – this

One Life

will teach you,' she shouted through the bedroom door.

It was Saturday evening, and Guy Fawkes night. I had been invited round to Sylvia's and I sat on my bed wistfully thinking what fun it would have been. Opening my bedroom window, I could hear voices and laughing from over on the bomb-site where they would be preparing the street bonfire. Doris spotted me and shouted up to me to come and join them. I shouted back that I was locked in. She went to get her mum and dad who shouted up to me, 'How long is your mum gone for?'

'Until tomorrow.'

'Right,' Sylvia's mum said to her dad. 'What a bitch! She ought to be locked up herself, that woman.' And with that she sent Sylvia's dad to fetch a ladder.

'You're not going to stay up there,' he said, as he came up the ladder to help me whilst other's held it steady. It was great being able to join in all the fun. Afterwards, I returned up the ladder and into my room after a jolly good night during which I'd shared baked potatoes and sausages with everyone else.

Most of my punishments came about because I had not completed my jobs properly or for answering back. My favourite retort was: 'I didn't do it,' when my mother accused me of doing something I had been told not to do (or which I'd forgotten which I often did!) 'Why can't I?' was guaranteed to bring forth a stream of verbal abuse, or a clout if she could catch me as I ducked and dived.

Once my mother asked me why I wasn't eating the boiled egg I'd been given.'

'I'm not hungry,' I replied.

When told, 'Get on and eat it,' I just sat there.

'Eat it or you will get it for every meal until you do,' she said.

I just sat there sullenly. The egg was presented to me at every

Growing Up

meal for two days. I watched my mother eat a good meal whilst I sat with this – by now, not very appetising – egg in front of me. By this time I was determined not to eat it.

In exasperation my mother then meted out the punishment I dreaded most. I was made to climb into the coal hole at the side of the sink. To do this I had to get up onto a chair and open a trap door in the wall. Inside it the coal hole was pitch black and I knew that there was a mousetrap set in it, for it was my job to put the dead mice in the dustbin. My imagination would run riot whilst I crouched, terrified, in that awful hole.

'I'm sorry Mummy, I'm sorry Mummy. Please let me out – I'll eat the egg, I promise.' She let me out. I ate the egg and was promptly sick and this got me another good hiding.

I have never believed in forcing children to eat anything due to this incident.

Sometimes I'd scream out and a neighbour would shout, 'Leave the poor little beggar alone,' but I soon learned not to scream out, as all it got me was another clout.

To some extent I did learn the warning signs that my mother's temper was rising. I'd see the twitching along her cheekbone, and when she was sitting down, her foot would start to bounce up and down. But she could still be very unpredictable. Sometimes she'd arrive home, or come off the telephone, in a temper and I noticed that one relative in particular, my Aunt Winnie, always seemed to wind her up.

My mother had got a big black cat to get rid of the mice, and besides being a good mouser, he was a great comfort to me. I'd sit on the stairs talking to this cat and telling him all my problems. Cuddling and stroking him made me feel a lot better. Whisky the cat was a true friend. I'd dress him in doll's clothes and take him out in the pram bought for me by Auntie Emma.

One Life

One day, when feeling particularly unhappy after a thrashing, I decided to run away to Auntie Emma's, so I set off to walk to Nottingham. The sun was shining, it was a beautiful day and people were busy about their tasks, smiling and chatting. Walking over the bridge towards Tooting Broadway I began to feel happy and contented. There was much to see and the birds were singing.

Now, where was Nottingham? I knew it was a long, long, way off. I'd gone there on a train once. Would Auntie Emma really want me? Was I bad? I began to have doubts about this journey. I felt sure I couldn't walk all the way to Nottingham and had no money for train fares. Was I really bad? My mother kept saying I was. Maybe I did not deserve her to love me. I decided I would really try to be good.

'I know what I'll do,' I told myself. 'On Sunday, I'll pray to God to help me.' I'd say my prayers properly like Aunt Emma had taught me, before getting into bed. I walked and walked until I could not walk anymore, and then I turned round and walked back home, determined to be better behaved.

I went to church each Sunday morning and to choir practice on Tuesdays. I thought the vicar was a wonderful person and the choirmaster was great. I believed in God and could talk to Him and tell Him my problems, and I always remembered to say, 'Only if it is Thy will.' I'd learnt a lot from Auntie Emma.

I did so enjoy the Guides, setting off in a furniture lorry to the weekend camps where we'd learn to pitch our tents, make campfires and cook safely out in the countryside. The St John Ambulance stretched me even further. There I learned first aid, home nursing, and how to handle accidents and emergencies. This was the first really interesting contact I'd had with learning and the fun of taking part in competitions and taking exams for certificates. For the first time I actually managed to excel and

Growing Up

nursing became the single most important ambition in my life. I have a couple of the original first aid certificates to this day.

I spent a good deal of time looking after the neighbour's children, playing and fussing over them. I loved them to bits, but if my mother caught me with them she'd just mock and make fun of me. Nevertheless the neighbours' trust in me gave me confidence in my ability to care for these little ones.

Then a friend at school introduced me to the Peckham School of Dance and Drama. This dancing school taught me a great deal besides ballet and tap dancing. It also taught me about developing a stage presence which, once again, did much for my self esteem. The school had contacts within the theatre agencies, and later on fixed up stand in jobs on stage for me.

I also went skating at Streatham Ice rink which I found exhilarating. I also found a boy friend who was a keen ice-hockey player. I was now thirteen years old and, though still enjoying school life to the full, would, on occasion, be asked by teachers about the odd black eye and bruises I'd suffered. My usual response was that I had bumped into a door handle, fallen down the stairs, or banged myself on the furniture. I never spoke about my mother's beatings to anyone.

Art was another subject I particularly enjoyed. My art teacher was impressed and gave me special lessons to prepare me for the exam. This was marvellous and for once my

Me, skating.

One Life

mother became interested in my passing this exam. So, perhaps purely from badness, I decided I didn't want to do art and didn't put my best into it. For the first time I'd found something that I could be in control of, and anyway, I wanted to be a nurse. As a result I didn't reach the required standard to gain entrance to an art college. I also became interested in classical music at this time and the music teacher brought in records to listen to with her at playtime.

It was about this time that I also decided I liked reading. The book that started me off was *Where the Rainbow Ends*. I read it again and again. My teacher caught me reading this instead of taking part in the lesson and asked me to read it to her at the end. She was surprised at the sudden improvement in my reading and asked me if someone was giving me lessons. 'No', I said.

After this the headmaster asked my mother to call in and she arrived with me at his office a few days later. The headmaster told her he was puzzled. I was well behind in my school work and yet it appeared that I had suddenly taught myself to read. I was horrified at my mother's reply. She said, 'She used to be very bright and clever. She could read before going to school but then she got meningitis. When she came out of hospital after being in for months, she'd become a dim, badly behaved and a wicked child.'

Then, when the headmaster suggested I have some tests with their school psychologist, my mother simply replied, 'I don't see it doing any good, but you can do what you like.'

I was mortified to have this said to the headmaster in my presence. I was not shocked at being called 'dim' or 'mad', as these words had been thrown at me so many times, but it was news to me that I'd been in hospital for months with meningitis. It must have been really bad for me to have been kept in for

Growing Up

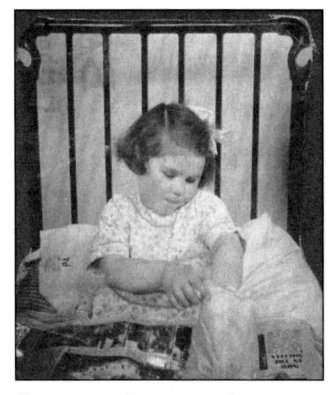

I managed, years later, to get hold of these two photos that my stepfather had taken of me in hospital.

months. Perhaps I *was* mad...

My mother took me to a large converted house to see the psychiatrist. I took a number of tests. I had to write down the definitions of words and there were problems for me to work out. Then I was asked if I wanted to play with a doll's house and I replied, 'No, I'm too old for that.' When told to paint a picture showing an angry scene I drew a picture of a mother in front of a red fire hitting a child over the head with a frying pan. He pinned the picture on the wall whilst the paint was still wet, and so I told him he was stupid as the colours were running. He laughed and took it down.

During six following visits I was asked searching questions about my home, my mother and other relatives:

I was asked to say which were my favourite colours and which relative would I put that colour to. Turning to him I said, 'I know what you are trying to do, and I'm not going to tell you anything!'

'What do you feel about yourself?' he asked.

'I'm dim, not good at much at school.'

27

One Life

'That is nonsense. You have a well above average IQ. Remember that and do not believe anyone who says that you're dim. You should believe in yourself and try and learn as much as you can. You could do really well if you wanted to – you are neither mad nor bad!'

Then he asked me about reading and I said I that I enjoyed it and had books from school to read. He pointed out how well I had been doing at the St John Ambulance, the Guides, and church, and how much everyone liked me. I was surprised he knew so much about me and he gave me a telephone number in case I ever felt I needed help. I was to hide it somewhere safe.

'And tell your music teacher, Miss Matthews. You like her don't you?'

'Oh yes, I do like her, because she brings in records I love to listen to *The Warsaw Concerto, The Four Seasons* by Vivaldi, *The Nuns Chorus*, and *The Dance of the Fairies* from *The Nutcracker Suite,*' I said breathlessly.

'Good, so you will speak to her then if you are unhappy about anything? You will you do that for me?'

'OK,' I replied.

He then called my mother in and told her what he had told me. She retorted, 'This place is a load of rubbish. It's just making her worse. You and your kind should mind your own business. She's not coming again!'

My visits to this house for these tests and the talks with this child psychologist proved to be the most significant and important event of my early years. I had been given information about myself that I could cling to and believe in. He was an important man with all the right qualifications. I realised that he had been trying to get me to talk about my mother and my life with her. I was not quite sure where it was all going to lead, but

Growing Up

what I did know was that I was getting an even more difficult time at home. Even though I couldn't understand why my mother was so convinced I was dim, there was also in me an unflinching loyalty towards her. I just wanted her love and approval. I wrote the phone number the psychiatrist had given me under the dining room mantelpiece in very small print so that it could not be seen without crouching down and looking hard for it. The room was redecorated later that year and so the number was lost.

I met some of my close relatives infrequently following the end of the war and some I still haven't met to this day. Aunt Winnie lived in a three bedroom well furnished flat in Westminster and her younger sister Betty lived with her. Later I was to find out that they were in fact my mother's stepsisters as they had different fathers.

Betty, as her photo shows, was a real beauty with a tall, willowy figure and long wavy hair, and she had an attractive

Above: Auntie Winnie.

Right: Auntie Betty.

One Life

gentle nature which shone out from her face. She was becoming well known as a model in London and I hero-worshipped her.

Auntie Winnie always seemed to speak in derogatory manor about my mother and there was constantly tension between them. Sometimes I'd do some cleaning for her, and she'd give me a couple of bob, but although she was nice enough towards me I always felt there was some distance between us.

On one occasion I'd overslept and my mother was banging about shouting, 'I'll show her – lying there in bed, the lazy little bitch.' A shoe was thrown at my head and I got up only to find I was locked in my room. This meant I'd be missing an important sports day in which I'd been entered in the high jump for the St John Ambulance team. I felt that I was letting them down badly and begged my mother to let me go. She shouted even more loudly, 'It serves you right. You'll get up in future won't you!'

I sat on my bed, hating her, feeling so miserable. What had I to do to get her to even like me? I wished my Dad were alive. It would be different then. I knew it would.

I lay on my bed remembering the time I had been jeered at by a girl walking along behind us on our way home from school saying, 'You didn't lose your Dad in the war. You just never had a dad did you?'

'I did have a Dad,' I said, 'but he died. He was going to be a doctor, but he died.'

'If you did have a Dad, he must have gone up on a balloon then into the sky, so there!'

'That's it, don't you call my Dad. Put your fists up.' She was bigger than me but I didn't care. I dumped my plimsoll bag onto Sylvia, and said, 'Come on then.'

She swiped out at me but I ducked and landed her one. A couple of boys passing by shouted, 'Come on Titch, give it to her!'

Growing Up

This egged me on. She went for me again but I had good reason to be very quick at ducking. Now I landed her one right on her nose and, at this, she ran off. I collected my plimsoll bag from Sylvia and we walked on home.

From eleven to thirteen years of age I had a few fights over never having had a father, whereas if you'd you lost your dad in the war, he was a hero. I also got picked on occasionally as my mother's life style was questionable. Other kids would say nasty things about her and I'd stick up for her. Although I did not go looking for fights I could, and did, stand up for myself.

'This punishment is just so unfair,' I said to myself as I lay there feeling miserable. I just didn't feel like doing anything and kept thinking about the team and wondering about how they were doing. It began to get dark and I lay there with my eyes closed, thinking about what it would have been like if my father were alive.

When I awoke next day I was determined to leave home. I'd go and see Aunty Winnie. She'd help me, and maybe I could live with her. I'd got very little money, so I'd walk there. I walked the route that I had before, only this time I was walking from Mitcham to my Aunt Winnie's in Vauxhall, Chelsea, never to return home again.

I walked along the main road to Tooting Broadway, then on to Tooting Beck. I went via the underground stations: Clapham Common, Balham, The Elephant and Castle, and onto and over Vauxhall Bridge. I don't know how many miles it was, but I enjoyed the challenge of the walk and stopped to look at places and things which took my fancy. I don't know what I expected my Aunt to say, or even if she would be in.

I arrived exhausted. My walk had taken me all day and it was now well into the evening. I tried to tell Aunt Winnie why I had run away, how unhappy I was, and that my mother hated me.

'She will be glad to be rid of me,' I said.

She said I could stop the night but must go home the next day as she couldn't get involved. She added that my mother would say she had enticed me away deliberately. She then rang my mother and told her what I had said in full. I felt betrayed, and so very tired, and now I knew I'd be in for a thrashing as well when I did get home. I could not help dwelling on how I had been let down. Maybe, I thought, I'd be better off without relatives. 'I've just got to get away from home,' I whispered, as I clambered wearily into bed and drifted off into an exhausted sleep.

Little did I know of the revelation that was to befall me the next day.

Chapter Four

A Shocking Revelation

I set off the next day with a heavy heart. I knew I was in for trouble when I got home.

'I'm going to leave home for ever,' I said to myself.

I was not sure how you went about leaving home and living on your own. So on my way, I decided to call in at the police station and inform them of my intentions. I'd do it properly this time, and they'd tell me what to do. One thing I was sure about: I was definitely leaving home!

The bobby at the police station listened to me patiently, and then said, 'You can't leave home just like that. How old are you?'

'I'm fourteen,' I replied.

'Well, you have to be eighteen before you can leave home,' he said.

My heart sank, four whole years before I could leave home; there was no way I could wait that long!

'But my mother hates me!' I said.

'Tell you what Love, I will go and get a woman police officer. You can talk to her about your problems. Would you like a drink while you wait?'

'Yes, please.'

The woman police officer came, took me into a side room, and asked me why I wanted to leave home. I was wary, and so I just said I was very unhappy, my mum didn't want me. In fact, she hated me.

One Life

'I'm sure she doesn't really hate you. What makes you think that she does?'

'I just know she hates me,' I repeated.

'Tell you what, this police officer and I will take you home and you can talk it through with your mother. How will that be?'

At this I became very agitated. 'No, I had better go on my own,' I stammered hurriedly.

I was terrified what my mother would do to me, arriving home with these two coppers in tow. However, there was no getting out of it now. They were quite insistent. I'd have run if I could, especially when we arrived at my front door. The policeman rang the bell. Should I bolt for it? Too late! She was there. She looked at the policeman.

'What's she done?'

It was the policewoman who answered: 'Oh, don't worry. She hasn't done anything wrong. She just said that she wanted to leave home, so we said we would bring her back and have a chat.'

But my mother was in no mood for chatting. She grabbed me, clouted me around the head, dragged me inside and slammed the door in the coppers' faces. Then she pushed me up the stairs, along the landing, and in through the kitchen. I had my arms up, covering my head, as I crouched forward, fending off the blows. Finally I managed to break away from her and ran into the front room, but she chased me round the table and back into the kitchen. Now, out of breath, she shouted to me to get to my bedroom. I did so willingly, and she locked me in. I was panting, but at least I was safe for the moment.

It wasn't long before I heard her on the phone. She was ringing my Aunt Winnie to tell her what I'd done.

'She's an ungrateful little bastard, that's what she is, a bastard.

A Shocking Revelation

It's high time she knew that George isn't her father. She doesn't deserve to have his name.'

I had been standing, leaning against the wall, listening to her deliberately loud conversation. I gasped, incredulous at what I had just heard. It was like being punched in the stomach. The father figure that I had idolised, and wanted to follow in my career, was apparently not my father! I slid down the wall and slumped to the floor. I could feel the last remnants of my world falling apart. Oh, God, I thought, I am a bastard. I am that dreadful word that she had called me so often. I had built my life around the image of my dad, George, as I had believed him to be, hoping that I took after him more than my mum. Now my illusion was shattered. And it was my mother who had brought my world crashing down.

I sat there for a long time after she'd finished on the phone. First dusk arrived and then darkness came. I felt myself sinking into an abyss of confusion and panic. Who am I? Is this why she hates me? Who is my father? Not Old Nick, surely? Not Edward?

I felt sick. It is impossible for anyone who has not gone through this experience, especially back then, to imagine what it feels like to have the world wrenched from you. Hearing the word 'bastard' uttered in such a spiteful way by my own mother was just so cruel. I was so ashamed. Did everyone know I was a bastard? Shame, revulsion, and fear about just who my father might be, these emotions all whirled around in my head. I sat there for a long time, numb, not wanting to move. Eventually I managed to crawl into bed, and, cold and stiff, I cried myself to sleep.

The next morning I could hardly look at my mother, and when I did it was with contempt. I just wanted to get away from her, to

One Life

go anywhere, to just walk and walk and never come back. Feelings of anger, shame and hatred were so intense inside me. Fortunately for me she had a rush order ready for me to deliver to a customer in London: a satin dressing gown for a customer's daughter who was going into hospital the next day.

Walking to the Underground station I thought about my aunts again; surely they would know who my real father was? I delivered my mother's order and then called round to Aunt Winnie's flat again, hoping that she would not mention yesterday's incident. I would just work my way round to asking about my father. As it turned out, I found my Aunty Cissy was there too. Aunt Winnie's flat functioned as a meeting place for family members.

Auntie Cissy was shorter than the other sisters, although taller than my mother. She had mousy hair. Nothing about her made her stand out in a crowd, but she was very intelligent and had a responsible job in the Civil Service. It was left to Auntie Cissy, being the youngest, to look after my Nan, who I was not to see for some time, although the reason for this would not become clear until later. There were only about five years, as far as I know, between Aunty Cissy and myself, although the gap appeared very wide at that time.

I did not quite know how to broach the subject of my father. However, Cissy could obviously see I was upset. She asked me what was wrong. I told her that

Auntie Cissy

A Shocking Revelation

I had heard my mother's conversation to Aunt Winnie on the phone the day before. 'You poor little sod, how could she do that to you?' she said. Then, Aunt Cissie looked at Aunt Winnie, who, to do her justice, was squirming, and said, 'What are we going to tell her?'

'We can't tell her.' Aunt Winnie was looking at me awkwardly. 'But your father was a good man, a very caring man. You'd be proud of him if you knew him.'

'But why can't you tell me?' I pleaded.

'I just can't,' replied Aunt Winnie. 'There is a very good reason, but for the moment you will just have to take my word for it.'

'It's not Nick or Edward is it?' I cried desperately.

She reassured me that it was neither Nick nor Edward, and with this I had to be content.

My Aunt Betty had arrived while we were talking. She added nothing to the conversation, so I let it go. She had a gentle and unassuming nature despite being in her glamorous job, and would sometimes take me out with her, telling me to call her Betty, like everyone else did. Her fiancé, John, a Polish immigrant, was tall and very handsome with wavy blond hair. He had an identical twin brother, but there was something mysterious about him, something not talked about. I was never allowed to stay with them. I came to the conclusion he must be a gregarious, flirtatious rogue.

I did not see a lot of Betty because she was busy modelling. She was to tell me that modelling was not all glamour. In reality it meant changing clothes in a rush all day, always having to be meticulously dressed on or off the cat-walk, travelling a good deal, and getting home dog-tired.

Aunt Betty was planning to marry John very soon and my

mother was to make the cake and ice it for them. Rationing was still a problem and finding enough coupons for a rich fruit cake had been very difficult. I had my St John Ambulance meeting that evening, so said my goodbyes and left my aunt's house to go home. I did so wish I lived there instead of home with my mother. I thought about my St John meeting on the way home.

A camping holiday in Jersey was planned and my mother had agreed I could go. I was never short of money and was encouraged to go off to camps because it left my mother free of me. This was to be an exciting holiday. I was going abroad for the first time, staying at a Toc H hostel for two weeks. I was nearly fifteen years old and I was to leave school that term.

Me, camera in hand with a friend.

A Shocking Revelation

The long-awaited start to my holiday arrived. We travelled in a removal lorry to the boat at Southampton. Onboard we were to sleep on the deck over the engine-room. The crossing was very rough; almost everyone in the boat was sick, and the only two of us not affected were kept running around all night looking after other people.

We arrived next day to bright sunshine and screaming gulls. I could feel the excitement and anticipation rising in me as we got off the ferry and into the lorry to go to the hostel. Jersey was wonderful and the sands were golden. I was stunned by the magnificent rugged coastline, its beautiful bays and Saint Helier, with its holiday atmosphere and exciting shops. Life was good.

We found jewellery and things were much cheaper than in the shops back home. I bought my very first camera on that holiday: a Brownie box camera for seven shillings and sixpence. After buying a present for my mother I could not resist spending the greater part of the rest of my money on it. It was the beginning of a hobby that would stay with me throughout the years.

One Life

I took these photos in Jersey with my new camera before returning home in high spirits.

Not long after that, and on leaving school and getting settled into my first job, an incident at home was to precipitate my departure from home for good.

Chapter Five

Leaving Home

Those about to leave my school were always taken to have a look around Pascal's, the local sweet factory. I decided this was not for me. I really wanted to be a nurse, but I was too young and I didn't have the necessary qualifications. I was also told that I didn't have a chance of getting an office job. My mother said I was to get any job going, and be working at it within a week of leaving school, or I would be 'out on my ear'.

Visiting my aunts on the Saturday before my last days at school, I was sitting talking to Aunt Cissy about wanting to work in an office, and she said, 'If you want to do anything badly enough, you can do it. Come on, let's look in the paper.' We found a job for a receptionist-filing clerk, in an architect's office in Manchester Square (behind Selfridges in Oxford Street), and she helped me to write a letter applying for the job. I posted it on the way home, never expecting a reply, but to my surprise, and only a couple of days later, I did get a reply inviting me to attend an interview.

I rang Cissy and she said she would lend me a black skirt, a cardigan, a handbag and a pair of gloves. I had a pair of black shoes. Then I remembered what Aunt Emma had told me: 'Always have a clean hanky with you.'

I was a little nervous when I arrived. There were five other girls waiting. 'I won't stand much of a chance here,' I said to myself. In the event, I was called in first and I thought, This seems to be going well – even if I don't get the job.

One Life

Mr Welbeck, a good-looking, friendly man interviewed me. He asked me, 'Why do you want this job? '

I replied, 'I want to do something that would be interesting and at the same time involve meeting people. Architecture, houses and people all appeal to me, and I also want to learn to type.'

He then asked a few more questions and finished by saying, 'Thank you for coming. We have your details and will let you know by telephone if you have been successful.'

Later that same day, the phone rang. It was Mr Welbeck – to offer me the job. I was amazed and delighted. He asked if I could start on the following Monday and I replied, 'Yes please!'

I'd just two more days at school and then it would be the weekend. I whooped with joy. 'Yes,' I shouted, 'I've done it! I can do anything if I want to and I really try.'

I'd got the first job I'd applied for, a job that I had been told I could not possibly get. I needed this boost to my self confidence at this time in my life. In the future, whenever a challenge presented to me, I'd repeat to myself, 'I can do anything if I want to do it enough.'

My mother asked what I was shouting about, and I told her. I did so want her to be proud of me.

'Well, you won't keep that for long with *your* spelling,' she said.

But nothing could deflate me at that moment. I couldn't wait to tell Cissy the news.

I settled into the job quickly and my boss allowed me a day release each week to learn typing at the local tech. The secretary had patience and I learned quickly. We were given a bonus at Christmas, and a crate of champagne was brought in for all the staff to share when a big job had been landed.

Leaving Home

I was very happy and excited in my work, although I still wanted to be a nurse eventually. I kept up my St John Ambulance, doing duties at the local cinema at weekends, and I especially enjoyed the duties at the fair on Mitcham Common.

Aunt Betty's wedding was only a few days away now. My mother had made a rich, dark fruit, three-tier wedding cake, despite rationing still being with us. She'd made a beautiful job of decorating it, and Aunt Betty was coming to collect it in her fiancé's car.

A few minutes before their arrival, my mother had been talking to Aunt Winnie on the phone, and now she appeared to be very edgy. I felt a sense of foreboding.

She was now in one of her moods and I knew how quickly she could turn on people.

Then Betty arrived with her fiancé, John. I suppose she had been showing him where the flat was. He drew up nearby, stopping for her to get out, and she came and rang the doorbell. My mother, answering the door, asked where John was. Betty replied that he was parked just a little way off.

'My flat isn't good enough to park in front then,' my mother said.

Betty looked perplexed, saying, 'Come on, Elsie, John was not quite sure where to park. I told him that he was fine where he was.'

My mother took Betty into the dining room to see the

My mother's flat. My bedroom is the one over the front door.

43

One Life

cake. Betty was delighted with it and said so.

Then my mother asked, 'Where's John then? Isn't he coming into my house? Is my house not good enough to come in either?'

I stood there shaking, pale and apprehensive; I hated scenes like this.

'Look, I'll go and get him. He's probably just giving me a chance to talk to you, Elsie, for a couple of minutes before coming in to look at the cake and carry it out,' said Aunt Betty, over her shoulder, as she left hurriedly.

It was too late. My mother's temper was in full flow by now. She picked up the cake, carried it to my bedroom window overlooking the front door, and, just as they neared the door, threw it out of the window, screaming, 'Eat that if you can!'

The cake landed in front of them on the path. They just stood there, transfixed for a few seconds, and then, turning, walked back to their car and drove off. I ran out of the front door and down the street, desperate to catch up with the car, but knowing I could not. I knew I was going to feel the full weight of my mother's temper if I stayed. I didn't care anymore. I just wanted to get away.

As I stood there, watching the car disappear, my mother caught up with me. She clouted me and dragged me back by my hair. Neighbours, having witnessed the whole scene, were shouting, 'Leave her alone, haven't you done enough?'

Pushing me down onto my knees, over the remnants of the cake at the front door, and still holding me by my hair, she screamed, 'Pick it up you little bastard. You can have it for your lunch breaks next week.'

I struggled to scoop the pieces of cake onto the silver boards.

'Seen enough?' she shouted over her shoulder at the neighbours, as she dragged me into the house, pieces of cake

Leaving Home

dropping from the cake board as she slammed the door shut.

The temper she was in that day was the worst I had ever seen. She ranted and raved at me, picking on the slightest thing. And I was so angry at her for upsetting my favourite aunt.

I told her, 'Keep your cake. I don't want any of it.'

She went for me again, but I dodged her and ran round the table towards the door. A knife came whizzing past me and thudded into the door. At this I opened the door and ran into the kitchen where she cornered me. I grabbed her wrists and held them whilst she lashed out with her feet. This was the first time I had ever attempted to stop her from hitting me, but by now I was a little taller than she was. I have always felt very glad that I never hit her back. I feel that would have taken my own self respect away.

She stopped kicking me for a second. I let go and ran along the landing and into my bedroom, fearing what she may do next. Taking the key inside with me I locked myself in. In the past I'd had many things thrown at me, but this knife-throwing incident was a first and had really frightened me. I thought how near I had come to being badly injured or killed. The deep slit where the knife hit the door was still there years later. Eventually my mother went out and I was left on my own.

Opening my door warily, I ventured out. It was now 3 p.m. and I decided to leave before my mother came back. I phoned Aunt Betty at her flat and blurted out what had happened. She told me to come before it got dark; they would work something out. I took only the cotton dress I was wearing. I was determined to take nothing that my mother had bought for me.

Arriving at my Aunt Betty's an hour later, I found that my Aunt Cissy was there as well. Once I got inside I just couldn't stop shaking and I was sobbing uncontrollably.

One Life

It must have been all the tension catching up with me. They both put their arms around me, and, leading me to a chair, said that they would not let my mother ever hurt me again.

Aunt Cissy said they had telephoned my Great Nan who lived in Knightsbridge. She would have me until another place could be found for me. I had never met my Great Nan, and, although I didn't yet know it, there were some pretty obvious reasons why it was not a good idea for me to see my Nan at this time. I was told I should see her, and that she wanted to see me, but this would have to be later.

I felt myself calming down. They were taking over; they were making arrangements and caring for me. This was the first time in my life that someone had done this for me. I felt secure with them fussing around me, and I would be safe at my Great Nan's. My mother would not think to look for me there. Aunt Cissy said that, as I was under age, she would get in touch with a welfare worker that she knew. The welfare worker would look into my being allowed to live away from home.

Betty sorted me out some clothes and Aunt Winnie said that Jimmy would alter them for me. Aunt Cissy was to look in her wardrobe for me when she got home. They would drop the clothes in for me at my Great Nan's later. Aunt Cissy then took me to my Great Nan's house, knocking on the door and shouting through the letterbox who she was. Then, taking a key from under a flowerpot at the side of the front door, we entered a hallway where a light smell of musty lavender polish lingered in the air.

We walked through and into my Great Nan's parlour. It was full of old-fashioned furniture. A large old mahogany dresser dominated the room and there was a table with a heavy maroon damask cloth draped over it and an ornate lamp standing

Leaving Home

majestically in the middle. Looking round, I saw an old blackleaded range, its fire glowing brightly in the dimly lit but cosy room. By the fire there was a high backed chair and in it, languidly eyeing us up, was the biggest and fattest black cat I had ever seen. And, sitting in a rocking chair opposite it, was my Great Nan.

'Come on in,' she said in a welcoming voice.

My aunt went over to her, and bending down to save her struggling up, gave her a kiss on her cheek. I hesitated, but she beckoned me over, saying, 'Come on then. Let's have a look at you.'

Getting up from her chair with some difficulty, she hugged me, and gestured for me to sit in the chair with the cat in, whilst she collapsed back down into her rocking chair. Feeling somewhat guilty I gently encouraged the disgruntled cat to vacate his favourite resting place, and Aunt Cissy sat down on a chair pulled out from the parlour table.

Then, whilst leaning from her chair, and lifting a metal teapot from the top of the fire range, Great Nan asked Cissy to get a couple of cups from the dresser, and poured us both a cup of well stewed tea. She then exchanged with my aunt a few pleasantries about how her rheumatism was bothering her, whilst offering us biscuits from the biscuit barrel that she kept by her side. Fascinated, I gazed around this interesting room.

The huge mantle piece above the range had all sorts of nicknacks on it. Amongst them were old fading photographs and bits of paper stuffed behind an ornament of a man fishing. After sniffing around me and nudging me to stroke him, the cat jumped up on my lap, thus partly reclaiming his ownership of the chair. I wondered how my own cat, Whisky, was. My Great Nan, although quite frail, obviously enjoyed her peaceful world with

One Life

all her memorabilia about her.

Later, we went into a small room smelling of mothballs, which had been used as a storeroom for many years. We moved some of the pieces of furniture and boxes full of all sorts to one side so that I could get into the bed. Having done this, Cissy said she had to get back home and would be in touch tomorrow to see how I was. She said goodbye to my Great Nan, and left.

The following Monday I went to work, feeling a little apprehensive and not knowing what my mother might do. I told Rita, the secretary, that I had left home, was staying with my Great Nan for the moment, and that, because I needed a copy of my birth certificate, I would go in my lunch hour to the Records Office to get one. I did not tell her that my real reason for wanting a copy of my birth certificate was to see who my father was!

I vividly remember the experience to this day. On entering the Records Office at Somerset House, I paid the search fee and filled in the slip of paper given to me. The clerk directed me to a long row of red bound books on a balcony. I looked in the 'L's for LeCorney, my name on my identity card, but although I found my mother's marriage certificate I couldn't find one for my birth.

On going to the clerk to get help, she clucked loudly and asked what my mother's maiden name was. I felt myself blush, wishing a hole would open and swallow me up. She looked at me in a knowing way saying, 'Come on Love, what was her maiden name?'

I replied, 'Ralph.'

'Look over there, under "Ralph", and I have no doubt that you will find what you're looking for.'

I did: 'To Miss Elsie May Ralph, Domestic, a daughter, Margaret, born 12th August 1935.' I paid the fee of three

Leaving Home

shillings and sixpence and received the certificate.

Leaving the building in a haze, I made my way back to work. So this was why my mother disliked me so, but why did she hate me so much that she had to let me know about it in such a way? If George, who I'd idolised and wanted to follow by being a nurse was not my father, then who was? A bus narrowly missed me as I wandered across the road and this jolted me back to reality. I decided I must confront Aunt Cissy at the next opportunity.

For the first time I was a few minutes late arriving back at work. Rita, the secretary, looked at me in concern, asking if I felt all right. She said that I looked very pale. I said I had had a shock and that I was sorry I was late.

'Do not be silly!' she retorted. 'I'll make you a cup of tea.'

Her kindness made me cry and I blurted out what had happened.

'How awful for you. It's not the end of the world though, even though you feel it is. It's not your fault.' She asked me if I wanted to go home.

'No thank you. I'm all right now.'

The day soon passed in the busy, pleasant atmosphere, although I was always apprehensive that my mother might be waiting outside. Looking quickly to each side, as I left, I dashed for the tube, only feeling safe when I got on the train to Knightsbridge. I felt better now, knowing that I was on a different line to the one I usually took.

On arriving home from work, and opening the door in the same way as my aunt had the previous day, I walked diffidently into the parlour. Great Nan had a hotpot cooking on the range and there was a lovely, appetising aroma. She was nodding off in her rocking chair but, as I crossed the room, she looked up at me with

One Life

a welcoming smile, holding her arms out for me to get a hug. This was a new experience for me and it felt so good. I laid the table and we had our meal.

My Aunt Cissy rang as we finished our meal, saying that her friend was getting in touch with someone in my area as that was from where an application needed to be made. I told her that I had been to Somerset House and obtained a copy of my birth certificate. She said nothing for a while and then said she was coming to see me; it was time I knew who my father was.

After initial pleasantries, my Great Nan left us alone in the parlour to talk. Cissy clearly had great difficulty in divulging the information and was finding it extremely upsetting, but she had discussed it with her sisters and they had agreed that I needed to know. If the information came out accidentally and the newspapers got hold of it, there could be dire repercussions for all concerned.

She started by again saying that my father was a good man and that it had not been his fault: I should be proud that he was my father. He was very clever and was, she said hesitantly, looking away from me into the fire, also *her* father – and my grandfather! This made me her half-sister. My mind reeled trying to take this in – my grandfather is my father? Seeing my look of horror as I tried to absorb this fact, she said quickly, 'But he is not your mum's dad, he is her stepfather, and you must not tell anyone.'

So that is why my mother hates me: I have messed up her life, I thought. Aunt Cissy went on to tell me that it had been my mother's fault. She'd been 20 years old, had known exactly what she was doing, and my Nan had thrown her out of the house.

I heard all this as if in a dream. This is not happening to me, I thought. Once again she impressed on me that I should not

Leaving Home

mention this to anyone, not to anyone at all, saying:

'You don't want your Nan and all of us to be shamed do you?' Inwardly shaking, I agreed, saying they need not worry.

This then was the reason I had not seen much of my family: I was an embarrassment to them, the skeleton in the cupboard. Aunt Cissy said I was not to worry but to put it out of my mind now that I knew who my father was. She said, 'You should simply be glad that he was a good person, and carry on with your life. You must say nothing to your welfare worker or the court hearing about this. Indeed, it must never be spoken of again.'

I agreed and she left.

I believed what Aunt Cissy said about my grandfather and about it not being his fault. I'd received nothing but bullying at my mother's hands. If his daughters believed in their father then so must I.

The next day Aunt Cissy rang again saying that a welfare worker was coming to see me the following afternoon. She added that I would need to have time off work. I wasn't to worry because she would also get time off from work too and be there with me. I said I was frightened they would make me go back home, just as the police had done in the past. She tried to reassure me.

'You'll be all right. They won't make you go back home. I'm sure of it.'

The following day I spoke to the secretary again. She spoke with my boss and I was allowed to leave after lunch. I arrived at my Great Nan's, nervous and apprehensive. Aunt Cissy was already there. She explained that I would have to tell the welfare woman about my mother throwing a knife at me, and continually hitting me, or they would not have a case to let me leave home. She added, 'I've told her briefly about what had happened the

One Life

day you ran away, but you'll have to tell her about all the times your mother hit you, and especially about the incident with the knife.

The welfare woman arrived and introduced herself as Mrs Edwards. She then asked me lots of questions about home, about being hit, and about being on my own for long periods. Then she asked whether I was left alone in the house with male lodgers, or my mother's men friends, and whether any of them ever made advances towards me. I only remembered the one occasion when a man friend my mother had met recently had put his arm around my waist whilst she was getting ready to go out with him. He'd said that I was an attractive little minx, and I'd promptly brought my elbow back into his stomach, repulsing his advances.

'You little bitch!' he'd shouted.

Then my mother had arrived on the scene, given him a right mouthful, and told him to get out. She didn't see him again.

I told Mrs Edwards that I could look after myself. I wasn't happy talking about my mother. It felt disloyal. She assured me that she had to ask these questions if I really wanted to live away from home and that, though she'd got most of the facts from my aunt's, she had to be satisfied that I really did want to leave home for good reasons. Then she asked about the organisations I was in and told me to ask at work for a reference. I felt sure I was going to like Mrs Edwards. She appeared kind and made me feel safe and she said that she would find somewhere for me to live as soon as possible. She wanted me to be settled there before I had to attend at the juvenile court in order to be granted permission to live on my own.

Next day I talked to the secretary at work and she said I could get a reference from the boss as to how I was doing my job. She said she would talk to him.

Leaving Home

The following day Mrs Edwards rang me at work and said that she would call at my Great Nan's at 5.30 p.m. My boss had written me a good reference and he gave it to me before I left. He'd enclosed the first report on my day release and said, 'I'm very pleased with your progress in typing so far.'

I thought how lucky I was to have this job and to get my day release at the college paid for by the firm.

Mrs Edwards arrived at my Great Nan's soon after I got in from work. She'd applied for a hearing before the juvenile court and said I'd need to have a health check, including a test to see if I had been interfered with. I'd an appointment for the following Monday afternoon to attend the clinic.

She also had some good news: she had found a family wanting a young female lodger in Mitcham, not far from my friend's house, St John Ambulance, the Guides, and my church activities. She said she would pick me up after college and take me to visit them on Wednesday. I must meet the family, the Sanderson's, to see if they liked me and I liked them.

Friday pay-day arrived. I was nervous – worried that my mother would be waiting for me outside work, the only place she could get to me. The secretary noticed that I appeared nervous and I told her why.

She said, 'Look, let's pin your wage packet inside of your bra. You can go a little earlier this evening. Your mother doesn't know where you are once you get on the tube and so you'll be O.K.'

Thankful for her understanding I set off apprehensively, looking neither to the left or right, until I'd arrived at the tube and boarded the train for Knightsbridge. I offered my Great Nan my money, as I'd done to my mother, but she refused it saying I would need it to pay for my new lodgings. My aunt had, in any case, given her money for food. I put most of the money away in

One Life

a drawer in my bedroom to save as she had suggested. Over the weekend my Aunt Betty, with her fiancé, took me to see *The Mudlark* in London. I thoroughly enjoyed the film. It was marvellous going out with my relatives.

On Monday I attended the health clinic with Mrs Edwards. Nervously waiting, I could not remember the last time I'd visited a doctor's surgery. I was ushered in by the nurse and told to undress – then a doctor entered briskly, listened to my chest, checked my reflexes, and asked me about my general health, sounding my chest and checking my reflexes. Then he told me to get up on the couch. I was frightened and hesitant.

'Come on, I haven't got all day,' he said, and examined me roughly.

I was terrified and the examination was painful. Then, sounding very surprised, he said to the nurse, 'This one is a virgin.'

He peeled off his gloves and threw them into a bin on his way out. By this time I was in tears. I had never been so embarrassed and ashamed. As I walked out of there, feeling so very miserable, I felt that everyone must be looking at me. I waited outside for Mrs Edwards. She asked me if I was all right.

I replied, 'Get me away from this place as soon as possible please.'

I sat in her car, tears running down my face. She said she understood that it must have been an ordeal me. I have never forgotten that awful experience at the hands of such a callous doctor.

The following Wednesday Mrs Edwards took me to see Mr and Mrs Sanderson and their son Matthew who was in a wheel chair. They showed me a small box room upstairs which, although plain, was comfortable enough and they seemed to be

Leaving Home

nice people. We talked for a while and they asked me about my job and my hobbies. Then they said that I was to be in by 10 p.m. at night, unless I had something special I wanted to do, and in that case they would need to know where I was. I would pay them £3. 2*s*. 6*d* per week for my room and board. This seemed fair and left me with £1. 17*s*. to pay for train fares and buy my clothes. I was to move in at the weekend.

I went back to my Great Nan's with mixed feelings. I was apprehensive about moving in with strangers but glad to be settling into a place where I would be safe from the constant fear of my mother's tempers. I still had to get the formal permission from the court and I was petrified about seeing my mother again. I also felt sad at having to say goodbye to my Great Nan who had been so willing to disrupt her life and take me in.

I soon settled in to a routine at the Sanderson's. They were a nice family. Even so I felt uneasy and I could not put my finger on just why. Later I was to realise that I had an uncanny sixth sense about people and, if I listened to this, it would never let me down.

Mrs Edwards visited a couple of weeks later to see how I'd settled in. There was to be a juvenile court hearing in a month's time. She told me that she'd had good reports about me from my St John Ambulance Captain, my Guide Captain, my Choir Master, my boss and my boss's secretary, and that now she needed to talk with neighbours, my school, and my friend's mother.

'You are not to worry about the court hearing,' she said. 'You have a lot of friends and there are many other people who think a great deal of you. Although you're only fifteen you've a good chance of proving that you're capable of coping with living away from home, but I still need to prove that your home environment is unsafe. You must not hold back, out of what I feel to be misplaced loyalty, from telling me the facts I need.'

This was very difficult for me because although I was very unhappy and frightened at home and hated life with my mother, I still felt an innate loyalty towards her. After all, she was my mother. But I was also very fearful of her. And I was scared stiff of facing her in court.

Nevertheless, I knew that I must go through with it all somehow.

Chapter Six

My Day in Juvenile Court

My day at the juvenile court had arrived and I was very frightened. The room I entered had a dusty, musty smell. In it there was a long table with people sitting behind it, and, facing this table, there were rows of chairs.

The first person I noticed, amongst those sitting behind the long table was the doctor who had tested me when I took my St John Ambulance exams. There were also a couple of other faces that I vaguely recognised, and this made me feel a little better.

My welfare worker sat by my side and Aunt Cissy was also there to give me family support. And, of course, my mother was present, together with some others, including a police officer and a press reporter.

The people behind the desk spoke to my mother first, asking her about the counter application she had made to the court to have me put away on the grounds that I was uncontrollable, a liar, lazy and untrustworthy.

'She needs to be put in a borstal to teach her a lesson,' my mother said.

'How much time do you spend at home with your daughter?' the magistrate asked her.

'I have to work but she is also at work so she is not often on her own.'

'Is Margaret left on her own some weekends, and even sometimes for a week, looking after the lodger?' the magistrate asked.

One Life

'No, she is not, and if she said she is, it's a lie,' my mother replied.

Then the magistrate asked, 'Has she been in any trouble outside of the home?'

'Not to my knowledge, but I can't be watching her every minute.'

After some more questions, and a discussion about my behaviour, my mother was thanked and told she could be seated.

Next I was told to come and stand in front of the desk.

'Margaret, were you really so unhappy with your mother?'

'Yes,' I said.

'Can you tell us why?'

Feeling my mother's eyes boring into my back, and panicking, I blurted out, 'She makes me scrub the step at six in the morning in the freezing cold.'

And then, suiting the action to the word, I froze and was silent.

'Come on, Margaret, there must be more to it than that. From what we have in the reports from the neighbours and the police we can see there is, so come on and tell us about it.'

It was no use, I remained frozen to the spot and looking down at my feet. I just couldn't tell them about the awful things that 'she', my own mother, had done. I was shaking and felt sick.

The magistrate looked at me reassuringly but still I could not say anything. The horrible silence seemed to go on and until, finally, all the people behind the desk started conferring together. Pale and shaking, I awaited my fate.

They were reading reports, shuffling paper, and I thought I heard one of them say, 'This women is clever.' Then the magistrate asked my mother if she would hand me over to them so that they could decide my future.

My Day in Juvenile Court

'Yes, put her in a borstal,' she replied.

'You are willing to hand her over to our care then?

'All right,' she replied.

I was then asked what I wanted to do and I told them I wanted to remain with the Sanderson's.

Then the magistrate said that they had received some extremely good reports about me, both from neighbours and friends, and from my work place, the St John Ambulance, the Girl Guide's and the Vicar.

'But you have given us very little information, Margaret,' the magistrate continued, 'as to why you want to leave home. The only information we have is in the reports from neighbours and the police. We will need to accept your obvious unhappiness, and your fear of your mother as the cause for your leaving home. Your abilities and good character are evident from the reports, and references in front of us and therefore we are going to make you a Ward of Court and allow you to carry on living where you are for now. Mrs Edwards has agreed to supervise you, and to give you help, should you need it. We understand you require clothes. A member of the panel has some clothes that she feels will fit you, and she will pass them on to Mrs Edwards. We all wish you well in the future.'

During this statement there had been an outburst from my mother and so she'd been removed from the room. Aunt Sissy said, 'My goodness, you have everything going for you now, all those people with good things to say about you. The magistrate and the bench were with you, so you just remember that in the future and it will give you confidence.'

I have remembered this and it has helped me through the years.

We went back to Cissies and she talked about me settling

One Life

down now and getting on with my work:

'You didn't think you could get an office job did you?' Remember you can do anything if you make up your mind that you really want to!' she said.

What an impact these words were to have on my life.

I found my job, which included reception, general office, and telephonist duties, satisfying and fulfilling. I also enjoyed the day release at the college, although my shorthand translation relied on good spelling and mine was not good. However I was employed at a small firm, with only a small staff, and this enabled me to gain the work-place confidence that was to stand me in good stead in future years.

I still attended the Peckham Dance School, where they had my name registered at an agency which provided temps for shows. This brought in extra money. I could earn as much for one show as I got for an entire week in my office job, but it was very spasmodic work. Every so often there'd be the need for temporary fill-ins and I'd get a call to go for a quick audition. Apparently it was all to do with unions demanding a set number of dancers per show.

The girls who were in the show full-time resented us stand-ins. As with my job, we earned more money per performance than they got in a week. They'd go without food to be in theatre; we weren't nearly so dedicated. Sometimes a scout would be in the audience and there'd be great excitement. I learned a good deal about what went on back stage, and about theatre in general, and this would be very useful to me in later years when I took part in amateur dramatics.

I carried on attending various organisations especially the St John Ambulance at Mitcham fair and the Festival of Britain carrying out senior duties. The vicar was supportive and he

My Day in Juvenile Court

I am here (on the left) with friends on duty at Mitcham fair.

introduced me to a Salvation Army home for girls with disadvantaged backgrounds. He explained to me that if they'd not been accommodated there the girls would have been sent to a borstal. Therefore it was, he said, quite usual for a Salvation Army representative to attend the courts, and he offered to take me along on his next visit to the home.

I duly went along, more out of curiosity than for any other reason, and he introduced me to the major in charge. She was a small, lively and authoritative woman with a kindly face. The major passed me over to a captain who took me into a back room where a woman was combing the hair of a young girl of about fourteen. The hair was wet and an odd odour hung in the air. The

One Life

woman asked me a little about myself and then introduced me to Doreen, the girl with the wet hair.

'Are you any good at cutting hair?' the captain asked.

'No,' I replied, 'I have never ever cut hair.'

'Well, now's the chance to try your hand at it. Her head is full of visitors, I'm afraid. We have treated it. You're not worried are you?' she asked Doreen, who, replied,

'I ain't if you ain't.'

I was appalled. 'Who me?' I exclaimed. 'You must be joking. I'm not touching hair with nits in it.'

'Oh a snob are we? Because if you are you won't be of any use to us.'

With this stinging remark, she put a bowl on Doreen's head, who appeared quite unfazed by it all.

'I'm sorry,' I said. 'I will have a go.'

I'd decided that, hopefully, I couldn't make a worse job of it.

My first attempt at hair cutting was not as bad as I thought it would be. I chatted to Doreen and found out quite a lot about her. She'd apparently been up in court for stealing and her mum was furious with her for being caught. Her mum had taught her to steal whilst being carried in her arms as a two year old. Doreen loved her mum and couldn't see why there was anything wrong in stealing. The Vicar later pointed out that, if that was what your parents taught you, then, of course, you'd never know any better, and that was why the Salvation Army believed that the girls in their care should not be punished but re-taught.

After this I visited regularly, joining in events, and helping out where I could. I painted faces on boiled eggs for Easter, wrapped presents, and joined them for the celebrations on Christmas Day. It was great fun when I too received a present. My previous experience of Christmas at home was of having a pair of slippers

My Day in Juvenile Court

slung in my lap at breakfast – if I was lucky! I remember going to Woolworth's, getting a cellophane box, arranging soap and hankies inside and tying a satin bow around carefully, only to have my mother sling it on to the sideboard.

I learned a good deal from the girls during this period. They told me about their life, and one, a very worldly wise and confident prostitute of fourteen years old, explained how her own father and brothers had initiated her into this career. She appeared quite unaware of anything abnormal in this. saying, 'I'll be back at it, too, as soon as I get the chance. It brings in really good money.'

I also attended a few Salvation Army services during this time. I liked the singing. The people who came certainly enjoyed these celebrations, which were both noisy and very physical, with lots of arm waving and people going forward to be 'saved'. It was expected that the girls would all want to be 'saved' and some would go forward simply to oblige. One day I was pushed forward, and duly 'saved,' although, when asked if I would ever join the Salvation Army, I replied, 'Only when I have one foot in the grave and the other is ready to follow.'

Sometimes I stayed overnight with Sylvia. The Fosters were like second parents to me; they would have had me to live there with them if they'd had a spare room. It was felt, however, that their house was too near my mother's.

There always appeared to be so many people crammed into the Foster's small but welcoming front parlour. After an evening out we often had jellied eels, or pie and peas at the pie shop across the road from the pictures.

The first months away from home flew past. I was now settling into the routine of working for a living and having full responsibility for myself. Although it was exiting, I sometimes

One Life

felt very alone – despite all that I was involved in. I would often spend my lunch hour at the Wallis collection, a private art gallery just across the road from where I worked. It housed a fine collection of art. I also loved wandering through Selfridges's, especially at Christmas time, looking at the high class goods being jostled amongst the crowds, and feeling the excitement of the festive season.

As time passed Mrs Sanderson became more persistent in encouraging me to listen to music with her son Matthew who was wheelchair bound, having had polio as a child. Matthew had a lot of classical records but he became more and more possessive and created when I went out with boyfriends. Sometimes I did enjoy listening to his collection of records, but he appeared to be developing designs on me which his mother encouraged.

I was beginning to feel uneasy within this home situation, and did not want to upset anyone, so I had a chat about it with Mrs Edwards at our next meeting. These meetings usually took place informally in a cafe. I told her that I felt that they seemed to hope that their female lodger would maybe become a wife for Matthew and that, although I didn't want to upset them, I would prefer to find somewhere else to live.

Mrs Edwards agreed, suggesting we give the need to find somewhere nearer to my work as a reason. I said I would rather live in a rented room somewhere rather than as a lodger with a family and she said that she would try and find somewhere. As I was still only sixteen she would need to look carefully at suitable places.

We met one week later. She had found one possible place where they had agreed to have me, subject to me supplying a good reference. It was a high-class hostel for girls who were at college, mainly trainee models, and near enough for me to walk to work.

My Day in Juvenile Court

We visited during my lunch hour the next day. The rooms were of a reasonable size with cooking facilities. There was just one, the smallest room, left. Meals could be cooked in the main dining room at weekends if wanted. There were six rooms in all, and two were doubles, with two girls sharing.

The woman in charge seemed nice enough: she liked me, and I liked the accommodation. It was agreed that I'd move in within the week and Mrs Edwards talked with the Sanderson's for me, which helped me to leave them on good terms.

I took to living in the hostel very quickly. The girls had refined accents and, since they found my cockney accent amusing, they encouraged me to talk. Although they weren't unkind, and they were fun, I decided it wouldn't be a bad idea to take some elocution lessons.

Miss Kent, the woman running the place, was strict, but she also showed many kindnesses towards the girls and me. After paying for my room and food I didn't have much money left from my wages and often ended up eating an evening meal of spaghetti or beans on toast at a Lyons Corner House that was open twenty-four hours a day and which was always warm and inviting. Frequently Miss Kent would say to me quietly that she had some food left over and could I possibly eat it for her – in return for some help with the washing up afterwards.

Looking out from my window I watched London go by. We had great fun at New Year. Those of us that had not gone home dressed up in fancy dress. I was the Devil and wore a satin cloak with a red lining and a hat with horns. We danced around Trafalgar Square to the midnight chimes of Big Ben, and when we arrived back at the hostel Miss Kent had warm mince pies and steaming mugs of cocoa waiting for us.

Although I was now confident and competent in my work, and

One Life

had been given a pay rise, my ambition to be a nurse had never left me. It was now one year before I could apply for nurse training. I did not have the necessary qualifications and wondered what I could do. Mrs Edwards suggested I use my St John Ambulance certificates and experience to look for a first aid job. She said, 'Perhaps you could try the Army, or the RAF. They train nurses and, although there is an entrance exam, I believe you could pass it now.'

I looked in the paper and found an advert for a First Aider at Spicer's Paper Mill. I went for an interview, taking my certificates with me, and was offered the job, although the wages were a little lower than my present ones. Rita and my boss said they would be sorry to lose me but, quite understanding my wanting to progress into my chosen career, said that they would give me a good reference.

Cash-wise, I was still able to meet my commitments, but had little left over. The work was interesting and always challenging. I dealt with all the minor accidents and kept a small storeroom stocked with first aid needs. I worked closely with the supervisor in charge of safety in the work place and together we were always on the lookout for any hazards. I missed Rita, and had felt very apprehensive at changing my job. But first aid had been part of my life since eleven years old, and so I felt comfortable with the job.

I was still making lots of enquiries about getting into the services to gain my nurse training and decided that the WRAF appealed to me. There was a medical training establishment at RAF Warton where six months was spent in the classroom studying for part one and two of the nursing exams. But there was also a stiff entrance exam in English, Maths and a General Knowledge paper to pass. The recruitment officer said I would

My Day in Juvenile Court

have to take 'another option' test in case I failed the nursing exams.

I discussed this with Mrs Edwards, saying that I did not want to be in the WRAF if I couldn't do Nursing. She pointed out that my identity card showed my name as LeCorney, which was not my legal name, and so I could probably use this as a way out if I needed to. I took this at face value at the time, but she was probably wrong. At the beginning of the war, when identity cards were issued, my mother had given my surname as LeCorney which was, by then, her married name, but apparently it was not mine – even though I'd always assumed this it was.

I had been in my new job for just four months when I sat the entrance exam for the WRAF on a cold bleak January morning. Exams posed a real threat for me. I had to remind myself that I had taken and passed several exams whilst in the St John Ambulance. I answered all the questions, left at the end of the time allowed, and was told that I would hear within a week if I had passed and been accepted.

Days passed and then I received a letter, hardly daring to open it. Another girl in the hostel had picked the letter up, and, when I hesitated, she said, 'Shall I open it for you?'

I nodded.

Opening it, and reading it, she said, 'There you are! You've passed! That's great, but we will miss you. Now the recruiting office wants to see you for a medical and to arrange your initial training at Wilmslow.'

I looked and looked at the letter, feeling a rush of excitement overwhelm me.

'Oh dear,' I said. 'Whatever am I going to tell my boss? I've only been there three months!'

One Life

Chapter Seven

Life in the Women's Royal Air Force, 1953

I arrived at RAF Wilmslow with mixed feelings of excitement and apprehension as snow was falling on a cold February day. I was ushered into a room with a number of other recruits. Each of us was assigned a billet, told to go to the mess for lunch, and then to assemble outside of the stores where we would collect our uniforms.

We were billeted in long huts, with rows of iron beds on each side, and between the beds there was just enough room for a slim wardrobe and locker. A round black-leaded stove stood in the middle.

Corporal Jenkins came out of her small bunk-room at the end of the billet and gave us a list of do's and don'ts: we must be up at 6 a.m. and make our bed rolls; the floor space under and surrounding our bed and the middle aisle must be kept shining and spotless; and, if anyone in the hut was not ready for inspection we would all go without breakfast. Any other rules broken by any member would be deemed the responsibility of us all and therefore it was then necessary to work as a team.

We walked across crisp, crunching snow to get our dress uniform and battledress, and three pairs of knickers (passion killers, we called them), and shirts with detached, starched collars. Then we collected our bedding from another store and, balancing this entire precarious load, made our way back to the billet where we made our beds. Putting on our uniforms felt very new and strange.

One Life

We soon became familiar with the routine. We marched and marched on the snow covered square until we could march every which way. Then each of us had to command the team in various exercises and work out strategies, both to lead and be responsible for others. At the end of a gruelling eight weeks, having passed individual and group tests, a ceremonial passing out parade was held, and I was given my chosen career choice and posting to RAF Warton Medical School.

Together with other trainee nurses I arrived at the Warton Medical School on a blustery spring day. The men had all, without exception, been called up on national service; amongst them there was a lion tamer, a butcher and a trainee vet.

After an introductory talk, a corporal showed me to my billet. As I was the only female nurse on this trainee intake I was to share with five other women who were in other trades.

After unpacking, I found the mess hall. I saw two lads from my intake sitting at a table and they asked me to join them. We introduced ourselves. Dave was of medium height with brown eyes and unruly hair and was quietly spoken. He came from Sheffield and he had worked in an office as a clerk He was very serious and studious and was to find no difficulty in passing the

Life in the Women's Royal Air Force, 1953

exams. Nursing had been the lesser of two evils for him. He was, he said, working his way up to becoming an executive. He felt this call up was an intrusion into his privacy and career.

Roland then introduced himself saying, 'I'm a lion tamer'

I laughed thinking he was joking.

'No, honest. Nobody believes me,' he said.

He was tall and slim with blond hair. My image of a lion tamer was that of a gypsy with a thick build, black wavy hair and dark skin. Roland was none of these.

He laughed and said, 'My family have an estate with an attached private zoo. We go on the road with the show in the summer months then return and winter at the estate, training and looking after the animals during the off-season.' He turned out to be a happy, devil-may-care but caring person. However, his general nursing suffered from a lack of serious attention, though being of high intellect, passing exams posed no problems for him. Here then were two reluctant medics.

So this was to be my entrance into the nursing profession. It didn't seem to be a very auspicious one from the look of these two fellow recruits. National Service had certainly increased the male intake, but it was a very reluctant one.

The next morning, nursing training started in earnest. The tutor introduced the course structure and told us about the exams we must pass.

'This is not just an easy option for those of you on "call up",' the tutor said, 'and so if you are not serious about the medical branch let the duty officer know. It will save me wasting my time. You will be having your first exam at the end of the month.'

I soon settled into the routine of study, doing little else apart from compulsory sports on Wednesday afternoons. Thus, tennis, as the photo overleaf shows, became my only outlet from studying and I took my text books with me wherever I went. The Friday before the exams arrived, we were told to go back to our billets and relax, as anything we had not learned now we would never learn. Nevertheless I picked up my books and the Corporal in charge of my billet found me.

'Still studying?' she asked.

'Well,' I started to explain, 'I really do need to study.'

'No you don't. You haven't taken your head out of your books for weeks. You need a complete break. You are going with Jean. She belongs to the Hostelling Association. You will go on a walking weekend with her and not come back until Sunday early evening – no arguments!'

Me, on my way to tennis.

Jean was a nice girl. She worked in the camp kitchen so there was no chance of revising with her. It was August, and the sun was out, and the walk turned out to be very invigorating and enjoyable. The sky was all-over blue and there were lambs in the fields.

Clambering over stiles, hiking through fields, and climbing up into the hills and then down into the valleys was all new to me. I was a townie and the only memories I had of fields and animals were from my days as an 'evacuee'. These happy memories passed through my mind as we walked. Jean was a tubby dark haired girl with a happy disposition and turned out to be a very interesting person to walk with.

Life in the Women's Royal Air Force, 1953

We chatted and laughed happily. She listened to my worries about exams and I listened to her tell me about her family and how she enjoyed being in the services. We stayed overnight at a hostel with other girls and they were all very friendly. We had soup and bread for supper, and a singsong with cocoa before retiring, tired and happy to our bunks.

We set off back to the camp the next day and the miles flew by. On arriving back, I had a bath and took stock of what was before me. I was much more relaxed and calm, and I had the Corporal to thank for that. The exam day dawned bright and sunny. First, we had a three-hour paper, with another in the afternoon, and next morning there was a two-hour paper on general nursing. The last written paper was in the afternoon and then we took our oral exams on the following day.

On the last day I went before a panel of three examiners who asked me questions about my six months studying, how I saw my career ahead should I pass, and what I hoped to do if I failed. Everyone went through this process. I was just so relieved when I walked out of the examination department for the last time.

Arriving back at the billet, I sat on my bed for a few minutes considering what to do. Well, I thought, I have given it my best shot, so I can't do any more. I wandered over to the NAAFI to see if any of my fellow students were there. I found Dave and Roland. We exchanged views on the exams and decided that we needed a drink. The nearest pub was at St Anne's, but the walk would do us good after being cooped up in the exam rooms. We had to wait until the end of the next week for the results to be posted on the board over at the medical school.

The day of the results dawned and it was my 18th birthday. Would I get the one present I really wanted, I wondered. It was another warm sunny day as we crowded round the notice board. I had difficulty in seeing anything, being shorter than most. Dave had got to the front and shouted that he had passed and was now looking for my name.

'Yes,' he shouted, 'you've passed,' and he pushed his way back to me and lifted me up into the air. 'Happy Birthday. Let's celebrate – have you seen Roland?'

No sooner had this name dropped off Dave's lips than Roland came out of the crowd saying, 'I've passed too!'

The three of us stood together, happy grins all over our faces. John, another lad we were friendly with, came up to us saying flatly, 'I've failed.'

We looked at him not knowing what to say, and he continued, 'I will go for the interview and see what my chances are of re-sitting it. If I can't, I'll have to take the second option as cook.'

And he wandered off disconsolately to the office to find out.

'Come on,' said Dave. 'Let's go and celebrate Margaret's birthday and our exam passes in Blackpool.'

And so it was agreed.

'Go on,' Dave said to me. 'Get yourself into civvies and we'll meet you at the NAAFI in half an hour.'

Off I went to my billet, and there, to my surprise, I found presents on my bed from the other girls. I was sitting on my bed, tears of joy and relief welling up in my eyes, when in came the Corporal.

'Well,' she said. 'Did you pass?'

'Yes,' I replied. 'What a wonderful day! I am so lucky.'

'Lucky my foot,' she said. 'You earned the pass, so open your presents.'

There were toiletries, perfume and a Happy Birthday card signed by them all. I was overwhelmed. I was not used getting presents.

Life in the Women's Royal Air Force, 1953

'I've been asked out by four of the lads,' I said, 'to go to Blackpool.'

'You're a quiet one aren't you,' she said. 'You don't do things by halves when you let your hair down do you?'

'Can you thank the girls for me and tell them that I won't be back until late. I'll thank them myself when I do get back. That is if you'll give me a pass to go off camp.'

'You go off and enjoy yourself,' she said.

So the five of us set off in a taxi to Blackpool fun fair. What a day to remember! We did the Big Dipper five times over, ending up at the pub for drinks. I arrived back late in the evening, flushed and exhilarated.

Next day we attended our final interviews and were given our postings and warrants to travel home on leave the following day. I was posted to Mountbatten, a flying boat base near Plymouth. I was to be attached to the Station sick quarters and was delighted. Little did I know just how soon I was to use my newly honed nursing skills.

I went to stay at Sylvia's house with her family for my leave and, on my arrival there, I found that Sylvia's Nan was very ill with cancer. The RAF extended my leave to enable me to help nurse her as I had put Sylvia's folks, the Foster's, down as my next of kin.

Sylvia's Nan had always been a feisty old lady, but seeing the change in her in such a short time shocked me. She was only able to take fluids with difficulty and had an oxygen machine at the side of the bed to help her breathing. I sat with her round the clock, washing her, combing her hair and gently talking to her. Sylvia's mum, in the photo, hung a hammock outside of the bedroom window so that I could get some rest and sunshine and yet be within earshot.

One Life

The District Nurse came in daily and the doctor called at regular intervals. He told me to call him if there was any change for the worse. I had never been present at a death; knowing her made it more difficult. During the next few days she became weaker and all I could do was make her comfortable and be there for her as she lapsed in and out of consciousness. Uncle George – the rich older brother of Sylvia's dad, himself a frail white haired, distinguished gentleman – came on several occasions to spend time with his mother. I took the opportunity to sit out in the garden and rest where I knew he would find me, and then we'd sit chatting. The family didn't like him much and said he only turned up on rare occasions.

Sylvia's mum

Then Sylvia's Nan lapsed into a coma and passed away quietly. I rang the doctor and then washed her gently, whilst all the while her eyes seemed to be staring at me. I tried closing her eyes but one of them would keep opening! Was she still alive and mad at me? I made sure both eyes were closed and then gently put pennies on the lids. And then I combed her hair carefully to make her look nice.

Sylvia and her mum were sobbing in the other room whilst her dad just stood there, helpless. Putting my arms around Sylvia, and her mum, I said, 'She is at peace now,' guiding them into the bedroom to say their good-byes. Dad Foster followed. I felt

Life in the Women's Royal Air Force, 1953

relieved when the doctor arrived and pronounced her dead.

He said, 'You've done a good job of nursing her and laying her out. It can't have been easy.'

These words meant a lot to me.

The family arranged a quiet family funeral and, a couple of days later, Sylvia's Uncle George took me to one side and thanked me personally for the care I had given to his mother. He said that he'd been doing a lot of thinking during the last few days. 'I have everything that one could wish for except a daughter such as yourself,' he told me. 'You, on the other hand, have nothing. I would very much like to address this by offering to adopt you. You would,' he hurried on before I could answer, 'be well looked after in my will when I die.'

I sat there in silence searching for the right words to express my feelings without hurting his.

'Don't answer straight away. Let me know when you have had time to think it over,' and with that he left.

After a while, I went back indoors and told Sylvia and her mum what Uncle George had said. This was met with a thinly veiled hostility. They suggested he must have ulterior motives and would want to take over my life. Sylvia's mum added, 'He is a sad old man who thinks he can buy people.'

'I won't accept the offer,' I said. 'But you are more parents to me than my mother has ever been.'

I didn't see Uncle George again before my departure for Mount Batten the next day.

One Life

Chapter Eight

Mount Batten

RAF Mount Batten in Plymouth was a flying boat base and I arrived there in mid September 1953. There were just one or two cotton wool clouds drifting across an otherwise clear blue sky.

Looking out over Mount Batten.

Reporting to the guard room, I was directed to the billet that I was to share with two other WAAFs. I would see little of them as most of my time would be spent in the station sick quarters. The girls were out and so I unpacked and freshened up.

As I was not required to report for duty until the next morning I decided to go for a walk. I found a public footpath and followed it along the cliff to Dunston Point. There I could see Mount Batten spread out below and a majestic Sunderland seaplane riding at anchor near the slipway. By this time the heat had gone out of the day and a cloudless sky was darkening to a deep midnight blue. 'I'm going to enjoy this posting,' I thought.

The sick quarters was medium sized with a fully equipped theatre for minor accidents. The MO, a retired surgeon, was a distinguished looking white haired gentleman with clear grey eyes. He lived off the camp and only came in on weekdays. In the evenings and at week-ends it was left to the duty medical staff to decide just who was an emergency case needing hospitalisation on the mainland, although we could contact the MO by telephone. The Corporal, a tall, slim man with thinning, mousy hair, was one of those people who tended to melt into the background. A regular, he had been in the RAF a long time, and had the medals to prove it. He was fair and easy to work for.

Jim, the male nurse, had enlisted to do his national service. He had deep blue eyes and a mop of blond wavy hair. This topped a handsome, warm and open face on which a quizzical frown would sometimes appear. He was a caring person, but as a medic he was hopeless. His background was in farming, and although

Me, outside the sick quarters

Mount Batten

he was quite able to cope with the exams, it was evident that this would not be his chosen career. We were kept busy with sick parades as well as accidents and injuries which called for quick actions and decisions. On one occasion we had a call to the quay where Sunderland seaplanes anchored. A lad had caught his hand in the winch around which a metal cable was wound which was used to pull in Sunderland flying boats. His fingers had been trapped under the cable and torn off.

Jim attended and, after taking the airman to hospital, he came back to write up his report. 'I don't really like this side of the job,' he said, 'and I'll be glad when my national service has finished.'

Later we had a call from the duty sergeant stating that a finger had been seen on the quay. Jim said that he was sure he had picked up all the fingers and asked if I would go back and have a look. I went down to the quay, dish and tweezers in hand, and just as I was bending down and picking up the dark blue black finger in my tweezers, the Flag Party arrived to pull down the flag. It was led by a Sgt Bulmer who barked out at me, 'What do you think you're doing?'

'I am picking up a finger,' I said, holding out the offending item. She came closer, looked down at it, and then, much to the amusement of the Flag Party, promptly fainted. I attended to her, and, once she'd recovered, she just marched off without a word.

I was to cross her path again.

Sometime later, when returning to my billet, I was greeted by one of the two girls I shared with, a bouncy redhead called Evelyn.

'Hello stranger,' she said.

'Oh – hello,' I replied casually.

'Sgt Bulmer is out for your blood,' she continued. 'She

81

One Life

reckons you skive off your billet duties.'

'That's because I'm on duty at the sick quarters most of the time.' I said.

'That's not what she thinks. She's not just after you though. You're lucky. She's making Pauline's life a misery. She's always after her, so much so that Pauline is a bag of nerves. She's always crying and just comes in and lies on her bed. It is affecting her work now.'

Pauline, a quiet shy girl, with brown eyes and jet-black hair, came in as we were talking. She had been in the service two years, and seemed to have enjoyed her job in parachute-packing. Now she just glanced at us, mumbled 'hello' and walked over to her bed where she lay down facing the wall. I went over.

'Are you OK, Pauline?' I asked.

'Go away,' she mumbled. 'Leave me alone, I wish I were dead.'

Sitting down on the edge of the bed I said, 'Come on, Pauline. Something must be wrong to make you feel like this. Evelyn has told me about Sgt Bulmer. She is after me as well.'

'Not like she is after me, she isn't,' she said, bursting into tears. 'She is hovering over me all day at work. You never see her,' she sobbed.

I sat quiet for a minute until her sobs subsided a little. Then Evelyn came over and said, 'Come on Pauline, talk to us. What has she been bullying you for now?'

Half sitting up, and twisting round toward us, Pauline replied, 'You don't know the half of it. I can't do anything right. She stands over me and I keep making mistakes. She jumps on me. I always did my job well before she started getting at me. I just can't concentrate with her standing over me, and now I've made a really serious one. I left a tab out when I was packing a

Mount Batten

parachute. It could have caused a death, and she's put me on a charge.'

'It sounds to me as if she has got you into such a state that you don't know what you are doing,' I said.'

'I can't do it anymore,' she blurted out.

'Report sick,' I told her.

'She's a bitch,' Evelyn said, 'a nasty overbearing bully. Just let her try it on with me.'

'Tomorrow morning,' I said, 'you report sick.'

'I can't,' she wailed, 'I'm not ill.'

'You are showing all the signs of a nervous breakdown and I'm not surprised with her bullying you like that. Come and see the MO.'

'I can't. I have to report to the Guardroom I'm on a charge.'

'Right. I'm going over to the sick quarters to ring the MO and ask him about taking you in tonight. I won't be long.'

Sgt Watts was in the duty room.

'Hi, what can I do for you?'

'I have come over about a girl in my billet,' I said. 'She is not well.'

'How not well?' he asked.

I explained, and he agreed that something needed to be done for Pauline urgently.

'You ring the MO, there's no point in passing it on second hand,' he said.

I rang the MO. He listened and then asked a few questions.

'Right – take her in,' he said.

I felt relieved and went over to the billet. Evelyn was sitting talking to Pauline who seemed a little calmer. I told her what the MO had said, that she was to come into the sick quarters and that we would look after her.

83

One Life

Evelyn said, 'Sergeant Bulmer can't get at you there.'

'We will both walk over with you. I shall be with you all night until the MO arrives in the morning,' I said.

She looked at me closely and said, 'I don't really know you do I!'

'No,' I replied. 'I spend almost all my time at the sick quarters looking after people. Trust me, the MO does.'

'I trust her,' Evelyn said.

We took her over to the sick quarters and settled her in.

The next morning the MO saw Pauline before sick parade. He decided to refer her to RAF Uxbridge for assessment and treatment. He told me that there had been complaints before about Sergeant Bulmer being a bully, but that the women were frightened to speak out. He then suggested I might think about specialising in dealing with people in a crisis situation.

A few weeks later I had a run in with Sgt Bulmer. I'd been called out to a WAAF who had been taken ill getting off the train. I was hurrying to get there when I heard someone shout out:

'LeCorney, come here!'

It was Sgt Bulmer.

'Can't stop sergeant,' I shouted back, 'I have a patient waiting.'

'Where is your hat?' She bawled after me.

The WAAF was sitting on a bench at the station. She said she'd got a stomach ache and felt faint. Whilst I was helping her to the ambulance Sergeant Bulmer came up close behind me and said, 'I want to see you now.'

'After I have finished seeing to my patient,' I said quietly.

The ambulance driver was standing ready to help my patient into the ambulance. As he closed the doors I heard Sergeant Bulmer shout after me, 'I'll get you, LeCorney, I'm not standing for your insubordination, and you're on a charge.'

Mount Batten

On arriving back at camp, the MO took over and later I told him what had happened at the station.

'That woman again!' he said. 'She has no right to interfere with my medical staff in the execution of their duty. Leave it with me and do not talk about it. Just do as you are told.'

I reported to the guardroom the next day in full uniform and was frog-marched in between two Military Police officers. I was very frightened and thought of the MO's promise to see I was all right. However, he was not with me and I felt very much on my own. I stepped forward and saluted the Duty Officer. The charges put forward by Sgt Bulmer were:

1. Improper dress in public,
2. Disobeying a direct order,
3. Insubordination.

I pleaded guilty to charges 1 and 2, but not guilty to the third charge. I wanted to say that it had always been drummed into us that the welfare of the patient came first, but I said nothing – as instructed by the MO.

'Do you have anything to say?' I was asked.

'No,' I said, and was sentenced to one week on 'jankers'.

This meant that I would have to get up very early each day in my best uniform and trot up to the guard room for inspection. I'd then have to do boring stuff in the guard room before attending to my normal daily duties. Then, in the evening, I'd have to do it all over again!

Where was the MO who had promised I would be all right?

I was being read out the rules and assigned my jobs, when who should come in but Sgt Bulmer requesting a female on jankers to clean out the woman's latrines. Oh no, I thought.

Then the duty sergeant said, 'Sorry, the only female I have is being assigned to the sick quarters. This is in response to a direct

One Life

request of the MO. He urgently needs a female nurse.'

Sergeant Bulmer's face was a picture, and she stormed out.

Arriving at the sick quarters I was ushered into the MO's office. He had another officer with him.

'This officer is from the legal department, Margaret, and I want you to tell him what exactly happened on the station yesterday.'

I did, and it was then suggested that I took out a Redress Grievance against Sgt Bulmer. The legal officer would obtain witness statements.

'Don't look so worried,' he said. 'You have a good team behind you here.'

The days passed and I served out my jankers in the sick quarters. Later I was officially notified that my grievance had been heard and accepted. All charges against me had been dropped and my record had been wiped clean. Sgt Bulmer disappeared from the camp and the MO said he was proud of me. The services had an efficient, quiet way of dealing with things. I felt relieved it was all over and remembered what it had felt like to be bullied by my mother.

Now I enjoyed my days at Mount Batten. Evelyn had received a letter from Pauline saying she was much better now but was taking a medical discharge. Her mum would be glad to get her home.

A new WAAF joined us to work with Evelyn in the cookhouse. Geraldine was blonde-haired, vivacious and fun loving; I liked her from the start.

Throughout this time, I had been working a lot with Jim, the male nurse. It was inevitable, I suppose, that Jim and I would become close as we spent most of our working hours together. He was very caring, and this was new to me. I clearly remember one

Mount Batten

warm summer afternoon. There was no one in the sick quarters and we were sitting outside in the sun, relaxing. Jim went inside to get cold drinks and then, coming around the back of me, he planted a kiss on the top of my head. Then he took hold of my hands, and, lifting me up out of my chair, his arms around my waist, he pulled me in close. I tried to turn my head away but he gently turned my face round and kissed me. I was taken by surprise.

'You must have guessed I love you,' he said.

I looked back at him. 'I knew you liked me.'

'Do you love me?' he asked.

'Well, I don't know. I think I do.'

Was this love? It wasn't quite as I had expected, but it was exciting to have his arms around me, and a wonderful feeling to have someone love me. Looking into his eyes, I said, 'I am lucky to have you love me, Jim. I will love you. I can't help myself.'

The days that followed were very happy ones for us. Jim phoned his parents in Devon.

'They weren't happy but they'll get used to the idea,' he said.

Soon after he took me out for a special meal; the restaurant had a warm, romantic atmosphere and we were led to a table with shimmering candles and small vase of summer flowers. Jim appeared comfortable and accustomed to eating out, but I thought about how little I really knew about him.

'For a farmer,' I said, 'you appear very adept at this.'

He laughed. 'Not all farmers are up to their eyes in mud all the time, or on the bread line. My family owns a large farm and holdings.'

Then I told him a little about myself. Looking at me with those deep blue eyes he said gently, 'Who your parents are does not matter to me. I am in love with you, not them.'

One Life

Then, putting his hand into his suit pocket, he took out a blue velvet box which he opened to reveal a ring with the largest sparkling white diamond I had ever seen, and, taking my hand, he solemnly asked me to marry him.

I looked down at his gentle hand holding mine, 'Yes Jim, I will,' I said, and he placed the ring on my finger.

We arrived back on camp feeling excited and happy. I showed the ring to Corporal Watts but he tersely suggested I did not show it off or a quick posting would be imminent, and that took the edge off my excitement.

Over the next weeks I avoided talk of future plans saying, 'We've plenty of time Jim. I've wanted to be a qualified nurse all my life. It would be a waste not to finish my training.'

I realised that, in the excitement, I had not given much thought to the future. Everything had happened so fast.

'You won't need to work when we are married,' he said.

'We should take our time. After all, you still have your national service to finish.'

'OK, I see what you mean, and we have both sets of parents to meet as well.'

I needed to talk more about my mother and how I had become a ward of court. I'd need permission to marry and who would I get this from? I explained the circumstances to Jim, telling him a little of my past life.

'What if we go together to see your mother?' he said.

'It has been three years or more now since I saw her.'

Inside I still felt afraid. I wondered just how she'd react. Would she create a scene? We got forty-eight hour passes to visit London and to make arrangements to visit my mother. We'd call in on the Fosters too, as I considered them more my family now. Legally, however, I believed I still needed a signature from my

Mount Batten

mother, or could the court grant it? It all seemed very complicated.

We arrived in London and booked into our hotel. Nervously I rang my mother's number. She sounded surprised. I told her that I was now a nurse in the services and engaged to be married. I added that I would like to come and see her and introduce my fiancé. She agreed to a visit the following afternoon. Replacing the phone, my knees shaking, I sat down. Jim gently took me in his arms.

'I didn't realise how this visit to your mothers would affect you. I have never seen you like this. You're with me now.'

We visited my mother as arranged. It felt strange walking down Heaton Road after all this time. My thoughts travelled back to the things she had said to me: I was no good, I was dim, I would not get a decent job. Well, I had. I had gone into a nursing career, and I now had a young man of my own. I began to feel stronger; she could not put me down or frighten me, I told myself. We rang the bell, the door opened, and my mother stood there. She looked us up and down and then said, 'You had better come in. Don't just stand there on the door step.'

We followed her up the stairs and in through the long narrow kitchen with the high window above the sink. I

Jim and me in London

remembered my grim childhood there. There was the dark, mouse-ridden coal cupboard that I'd had to climb up and into for punishment. A shiver went through me as we went on to the dining room where there was cake and a pot of tea waiting on the polished table.

This old familiar room still had an unwelcome cold feeling. I took in the old treadle sewing machine standing ready for use under the bay window, the faded 30s yellowing wallpaper with the three flying ducks on the wall, that fancy oval mirror hanging on a chain above the fireplace, and the lamp standard in the corner with its large faded and tasselled lamp shade. I shook off the lonely, unhappy memories as my mother's voice broke into my thoughts.

'So you joined the WAAFs then?'

'Yes, I trained as a nurse,' I said, looking at her.

'Like it then?' she asked.

'Yes, very much.'

I asked how she was keeping. She threw a sidelong glance at Jim before saying, 'OK, I suppose.'

I told her a little about the services, how Jim and I had met, and showed her my ring, at which she said, looking at Jim, 'Got more money than sense then?'

Jim looked her straight in the eye and said gently, 'I love your daughter. Nothing is too good for her.'

'Lucky her,' she said.

This had been the most that Jim had said, and, after a few polite pleasantries, the conversation petered out. I felt it was time to leave. In the past my mother could suddenly turn nasty, so I politely said we had to go but, if she liked, we could visit again. I felt very relieved when the door closed behind us.

As we walked away I gradually relaxed. Jim said very little

Mount Batten

and I was grateful for this. What a different welcome we had at the Foster's house! Arms were thrown around me and there was a hug for Jim from Sylvia and her Mum. Mr Foster shook Jim warmly by the hand. We were ushered into the living room. We spent a very enjoyable couple of hours and then left, promising not to make the next visit too far off.

Over the evening meal at the hotel I said, 'I don't know how I feel about my mother. I can't trust myself to be alone with her. I'm still intimidated by her. Why, when I'm mostly an independent and confident person, do I feel so insignificant in her presence?'

Jim looked at me with that endearing quizzical look of his and said, 'No one should ever feel like that with anyone. I can't even imagine what she's done to you to make you feel like that. Let's have a brandy to finish the meal and then we will have a walk before we go to bed.'

As we strolled along the Thames embankment on this warm summer evening, I thought how lucky I was to have the love of this handsome, loving and gentle man.

We arrived back at Mount Batten late the next day, tired but happy.

'Hello stranger. Enjoyed the weekend pass? Evelyn said.

'Yes,' I said breathlessly, 'it was wonderful.'

I held out my left finger for her to see.

'Wow, some rock – you're a quiet one! How long have you been engaged, and to who?'

I laughed, telling her it was Jim, the lad I worked with.

'You know they'll post you if they find out!' she said. 'They don't like engagements. They say it disrupts the service.'

'We're keeping it quiet, so don't tell anyone.'

'My lips are sealed,' she said.

One Life

Autumn and Christmas sped by and, before we knew it, Spring had arrived. One day, as I went in to the office, Corporal Watts held out a buff form for me to read.

'Well, it had to happen. You've been posted to St Eval.'

'Oh no! Is it because I'm engaged?' I said.

'I don't know. It could just be that they need someone urgently. It's a flying station – much bigger than this. If they needed someone urgently, this is the nearest place to come to. You must report there on Monday.'

'But it's Friday now!' I exclaimed.

'I know,' he said kindly. 'I have not told Jim. You had better go talk to him. He's in the duty room.'

I wandered out of the office disconsolately, and, entering the treatment room, I found him. 'Oh Jim, they have posted me to St Eval.'

Jim was devastated. 'We could get married and then you will be discharged.'

'I've to report for duty on Monday,' I said, 'which means I will have to leave tomorrow.'

Eventually the sick parade was over and I took the MO his coffee. Looking up from his notes he said, 'I don't want to lose you, Margaret.'

'Can't you do anything then?' I asked.

'Sorry,' he replied, 'but postings are strictly service territory. You have experience, and good reports, and they must have decided you are the person needed. You will be able to get weekend passes to visit Jim, you know. You had better go and get packed and then you can have the evening with Jim to say your goodbyes.'

I called into the office to sign off duty and collect my warrant for the journey.

Mount Batten

'Where is St Eval?' I asked Corporal Watts.

'Not too far from here. It's in Cornwall. Shackletons fly from there. You will be very busy: they have the occasional crash on the cliff-tops.'

I was curious despite my dismay at being posted.

Whilst I was packing, Evelyn came in from work. She stopped in the doorway looking at my packing,

'Blimey,' she said, 'where you going?'

'I'm posted to St Eval.'

'Good posting. Flying station, loads of men, oh but you already have one! What a waste! Come on, cheer up, and I'll buy you a drink at the NAAFI before you go to see Jim.'

'You're on,' I said.

And, the very next morning I left.

One Life

Chapter Nine

St Eval

RAF St Eval was a Coastal Command base situated three hundred feet above sea level on the north coast of Cornwall. Its runways surround the parish church of St Eval which is visible for miles.

After completing the formalities in the guardroom I strolled over towards my new billet. On the way I passed hangars, barrack blocks, administration and technical buildings and various wooden huts.

The camp was like a small town, complete with a post office-cum-grocery store, and a large NAAFI. I found my billet, and all three of the girls I was going to share with were getting ready to go over to the canteen for lunch. The first of them, Eileen, was a bubbly girl with green-eyes and freckles. She was short and tubby. Her hair was the closest I have ever seen to burnished copper, and she introduced me to the other two.

'This is Pauline and that's Dot, short for Dorothea.'

Pauline said, 'Everyone calls me Spanner. I work in vehicle maintenance.'

She was a well built, muscular girl with short black bobbed hair and was clearly not someone to get into an argument with.

Dot was tall, well built, and endowed with busts the size of hammock's which she carried in front of her with great aplomb. One couldn't help but look at her when she entered the room. Although not beautiful, she was good looking, and had the grace, bearing and confidence born of a good family background.

One Life

'Throw your things down on that bed over by the window,' Eileen said, 'and we'll show you where the canteen is. We can't vouch for the food though! '

'You're a medic aren't you?' Dot said, looking at my collar dogs 'It's about time they got another female nurse over at the sick quarters. Everyone's been complaining.'

We chatted on through lunch. They appeared to be a friendly bunch.

Afterwards I had started to unpack my kit when the duty sergeant came in and asked if I was the new medic.

'Sorry,' she said, 'but you are needed across at the sick quarters. You've not even had time to unpack have you? I'm Sergeant Murphy and they said that if you had arrived to send you straight over. Corporal Simpson has gone on compassionate leave.'

'I guess this is what you call being thrown in at the deep end,' I joked.

She grinned, saying, 'Go on, get on with you, and don't keep them waiting.'

I walked over to the sick bay; the MO had admitted a WAAF for overnight observation after she had an accident. I would therefore need to sleep in.

'Hello,' said the MO. 'Sorry about this. The patient appears all right, but I want to make sure.'

He looked to be in his late twenties and was about 6' 3" tall. His eyes, which had long, blonde lashes, were of the deepest blue and he had shiny blond hair too, even white teeth, and full, generous lips. He really was outstandingly good looking. 'Dishy' was what most of the WAAFs called him. Later I was to tease him about the length of the sick parade when he was the duty MO.

St Eval

'Your patient is in bed on the ward,' he said, and introduced me to Sgt O'Sullivan who, he said, would show me around.

Sgt O'Sullivan was an affable, kindly person who, as I found out later, enjoyed a joke. He was in his mid-thirties, had dark hair and was of medium build. Once I had been shown where everything was I went to see my patient before settling in for an on-call 'sleep in'.

The next morning I went to the office. Sgt O'Sullivan passed the report book to me and gestured towards another airman who was bending over a filing cabinet.

'This is Corporal Sugden, one of the few regular medics. Most of the others are on national service.'

The corporal looked up absentmindedly, said 'hello', and carried on with what he was doing.

I followed Sgt O'Sullivan into the duty room where he introduced me to three more staff members. Corporal Roberts, tall with wavy brown hair and brown eyes, peered at me from behind a pair of horn-rimmed glasses. He wasn't exactly handsome but the few tell-tale pockmarks on his face added to his charm rather than deflecting from it. He lifted one eyebrow and gave me a long hard look before saying, 'Glad to meet you.'

Then Sgt O'Sullivan pointed to a young red haired medic sitting at the table. I said hello and he nodded back, a mischievous twinkle in his eye. I found out later that he was an artist and that cartoons were his speciality. There was a large staff team maintaining the sick quarters and it included the ambulance drivers that were needed on this operational flying station.

I was kept busy due to the absence of Corporal Simpson who was the other female nurse. I rang Jim often, and told him I expected to see him for a weekend soon, but I was also enjoying the challenges of working with this new team.

One Life

As well as the morning sick parades, the family clinic, and the ambulance that responded to emergencies, both on and off the airfield, we also had a small mortuary. A most distressing job for me was laying out a young airman who had been pulled from the sea. His body was puffed up, with pieces missing, and his eyes staring sadly at us as we looked for his papers in his pocket. One had to have humility.

During our meal breaks we would chat about the day's events, both giving and getting support from each other, and this was how we dealt with any difficulties encountered during our duties. This spirit and support was to stay with me throughout the years. Team support and supervision of staff were to become buzzwords when what had seemed to happen so naturally in those early days in the RAF had to be given a name and taught in training years later.

I talked about how I missed my fiancé, how I was looking forward to my next weekend with him, and I was teased about my loyalty when I declined to join the others on a night out. Eventually I succumbed and agreed to go. There were five of us in all, three men and two women crammed into the one taxi. One of the men, Peter Roberts, got into the front and the rest of us crammed in the back. Another man, Michael, had invited Spanner and he pulled her onto his lap. I found myself on Corporal Sugden's lap.

'By the way,' he said, 'my name is Peter, off duty.'

I sat nervously.

He looked to me like a little old professor with his dark hair and thick black rimmed glasses. I'd caught him looking at me a couple of times – long inquisitive looks. I'd turned on one occasion and our eyes had locked. There'd been a sudden stillness in the air and time stood still. Then, dragging my eyes

St Eval

away from his in confusion, I had hurried from the room. Now, sitting nervously on his lap, I longed to get to wherever we were going and out of the taxi.

We had drinks, talked and played darts until it was time to go back. During the evening Peter kept close to me and I could feel a magnetic, exciting attraction between us. I thought of Jim and felt guilty, so I tried to avoid eye contact whenever I could, but I had to admit that I was enjoying the evening immensely and felt flattered at the attention.

We crammed into a taxi and headed back to camp with me sitting on Peter's lap again. Michael was engrossed kissing Spanner. I attempted to look out of the window but Peter's arm tightened around my waist and, despite my trying to loosen it, he pulled me round to face him and our eyes met. Then he kissed me full on the lips, a long lingering kiss, and I found myself responding, melting into his arms, and forgetting everything but this one moment.

'This is crazy,' I finally managed to say, pulling away.

'Is it?' he said softly, as we arrived back at the camp.

I scrambled out of the cab and, not waiting for Spanner, ran to my billet in confusion.

What had I done? I thought. I am engaged to Jim! Strange new feelings and thoughts raced around in my head as I got into bed. Lying there I thought, well this must be love then, this exhilarating feeling that had come over me when he kissed me, and the wanting to stay in his arms forever and never to break away. Oh dear, what a mess! Peter was probably just enjoying the evening and didn't feel a bit like I did, I thought, as I drifted off to sleep.

The next day, when collecting the medical notes for the MO's sick parade, I saw Peter leaving the office and my heart missed a

One Life

beat. However he just said, 'Hi,' and kept going. But then Sgt O'Sullivan asked me what I had done to his Corporal, looking at me with a mischievous glint in his eye.

'Me?' I said,

'Yes, you. He's usually quiet, but to-day he is positively uncommunicative and, from what I have heard from the others, you are the cause!'

I blushed and stammered out, 'Nothing, as far as I know. I'm engaged, remember.'

'Well,' he said, 'who are you trying to convince, me or yourself?'

I grabbed the files and fled.

The sick parade over, I went through to the duty room for my morning break. Peter wasn't there. Sgt O'Sullivan came in and I beat a hasty retreat. My thoughts were in turmoil. What was I to do? I didn't know how I felt about Jim now! And how did I feel about Peter? How could one kiss create so much confusion?

Peter and I avoided each other. Then on the Friday evening I was writing my report when Sgt O'Sullivan came in and sat down opposite me.

'Well, what are you going to do?' he asked, looking straight at me. 'Are you still trying to convince yourself and everyone else that you are in love with this young man you are engaged to?'

Then, looking at me with a concerned and kindly look, he said, 'You can talk to me if you wish you know.'

I sighed. 'I don't really know what to do. I realise now I am not in love with Jim, so I must be honest with him and break off our engagement. If I can enjoy being with someone else as much as I did with Peter the other evening, then what I have with Jim is not real love. I feel very confused.'

'Would you like a 48-hour pass to go and see Jim?' he asked.

St Eval

'Yes, please. I must go and see him, although how I am going to tell him I don't know. He is such a gentle kind and loving person. I feel so awful doing this to him.'

'Rather now than later though,' he said.

'It would be awful if I had fallen for someone after being married,' I replied. 'I'll just have to keep that thought clear in my mind when I go to him.'

I thanked him. Talking it through with him had helped me to confirm what I already knew I must do.

I rang and told Jim that I was coming to see him and set of with a heavy heart the next day. It's strange how fast one seems to get somewhere when not in a hurry to do so. I rehearsed in my mind what I was going to say all the way there. Jim met me at the sick quarter's swing doors. He put his arms around me and gave me a kiss.

'You sounded a bit strange last night on the phone,' he said, looking at me closely, 'are you all right?

'Not really,' I said. 'Can we talk somewhere private, Jim?' I had meant to lead up to what I had to say gradually.

'There's no one in the duty room. Corporal Watts is in the office typing an accident report,' he said, and so we walked on into the duty room. Then I pulled away from his attempt to put his arm around me and blurted out, 'Oh Jim, I'm so sorry.' The words tumbled out as if being said by someone else rather than me. 'I can't marry you! It just wouldn't be right. I'm so sorry. I just did not know what love is.'

And then I took my ring off and offering it gently to him, saying miserably, 'I didn't mean to hurt you Jim but I would hurt you even more if I went on with the engagement, and you deserve better than that.'

Jim just sat there, an expression of pain and devastation

One Life

crossing his face as understanding dawned. At last, as if it had been wrenched out of him, he asked, 'Why? What has happened? Is there someone else?'

'There isn't any one really. It's just I now realise that, although I care very much for you, my feelings for you are not true love. It was wrong of me to get engaged, I didn't know what love is, I've hurt you I know.'

He looked away, turning his back on me for what seemed a long time. I stood there helplessly, saying nothing, the ring still in my outstretched hand. Then, turning round with a controlled look on his face he said quietly, 'Please go.'

Dumbly I offered him the ring again.

'No, keep it,' he said. Then, seeing my attempt to put it on the table, he added, 'Please don't leave it here. Just go – please!'

I couldn't bear any more. Turning, I ran out of the room, down the corridor and out through the swing doors. I ran on until I could run no more, the salt in the wind mingling with the salt in my tears, and the seagulls were shrieking as if in anger above me, until finally I just collapsed onto a wall.

And I hated myself for what I had just done to Jim.

And I vowed that I would never, ever knowingly hurt anyone like that again.

So what was I to do now, I thought, as I gradually calmed down? Here I was with nowhere to stay for the night. I would need to get back to St Eval. Whilst on the train back to camp I reflected on the events of the past few weeks, the emotional highs and lows, and the chaos that one kiss could cause. Gradually though a feeling of relief came over me, knowing that whatever happened in the future I had done the right thing for both myself and Jim, however painful.

St Eval

I slipped unseen back into my billet. Fortunately two of the girls were on weekend passes, and Pauline was still out. So I had a bath and, emotionally and physically exhausted, I got into bed.

The next morning, a Sunday, I set off for a long walk and I listened to the sounds around me: the birds singing in the trees, and the children's voices. Cornwall is such a beautiful place. Slowly I began to feel more relaxed, and ready to face the world again, and by Monday I was refreshed and ready for work. What a priceless treasure it is to be young! Sgt O'Sullivan asked me quietly if I was all right.

'Yes, thanks: I have broken off my engagement to Jim It was awful but I feel better now.'

Later on that day he asked me if I would baby-sit for him as he and his wife had not been out since the birth of their baby.

'Yes, Sergeant, I would love to.'

'Then I'll take you across to meet my wife at the end of the shift. You can have tea with us.'

They were living in their own caravan on the camp whilst waiting to move into one of the married quarters.

His wife opened the caravan door and, kissing her on the cheek, he introduced me.

'Call me Sandra,' she said.

She was a petite woman, with long brown wavy hair and a warm welcoming smile.

'Jennifer is asleep but will be waking soon for a feed. We'll have some tea whilst we've got the chance!'

She had already made up three salads for us and, after tea, she showed me around their tiny caravan. It was cosy and spotlessly clean. Then baby started crying for her feed. She was adorable. Sandra passed her to me. I expect this was to see how I handled her. After a very enjoyable couple of hours I took my leave of them, promising to baby-sit on Saturday, so that they could celebrate their fourth wedding anniversary.

The next couple of days were very busy. The dental nurse was off sick. She'd been sniffing the gas, become addicted to it, and had been found unconscious on the floor. I had to cover for her until a new nurse was posted in.

I'd only had fleeting glimpses of Peter since coming back after the weekend. I felt myself blushing when I thought of that evening out, believing that it had meant nothing to him.

Saturday came and, after a trip into Newquay with Pauline, I had a quick bath and made my way over to Sgt O'Sullivan's caravan. Baby Jennifer had not yet settled. She smelled of talcum powder and I was delighted to take over and cuddle her. Her skin was soft and downy, just like a peach. Her blue eyes were fixed on me trustingly and I thought how dependent this tiny little human being would be upon me for the next couple of hours. Sandra showed me how she liked Jennifer to be laid in her crib and then they left for their evening out.

I was just about to put Jennifer in her crib when I heard a knock at the caravan door. Holding the baby in one arm, I opened the door with the other and looked out inquisitively: there stood Peter.

'Hi,' he said, stepping into the caravan, 'I've come to baby-sit for Jennifer.'

'That's what I am here for,' I said, surprised.

'I see,' he replied, taking his coat off and casually sitting down on the couch, 'and I suppose they omitted to tell you they had asked me to baby-sit?'

'No,' I said, 'they certainly didn't tell me.'

'Sgt O'Sullivan has obviously been doing a spot of matchmaking,' he said, grinning broadly, quite obviously not in

St Eval

the least put out about it. In fact, he looked rather like a cat with a saucer of cream. Looking down at Jennifer and touching her cheek gently he said, 'Hello there.'

I suddenly felt very nervous and shy and my mouth had become dry. 'I was just about to put Jennifer in her cot, I won't be a minute,' I said, moving away a little, whilst trying to keep calm and composed. I took my time with Jennifer, making sure she was settled, and this gave me a few moments to collect myself.

Then I walked through to where Peter was casually sitting reading the paper. Two cups of coffee were on the table and he had put the record player on low in the background. I recognised the song, 'When you are in love', sung by Mario Lanza, a particular favourite of mine.

Sitting down, and hoping that he couldn't see my hand tremble, I picked up my coffee. I glanced sideways at him and, without a word, he passed me the outside page of the paper to read. My heart was thumping and I stared blankly at the printed pages. He then carefully folded his paper, placed it down beside him, and casually put his arm around my shoulder. I kept my eyes steadily on the printed page as he moved closer. Then, taking the paper out of my hands, he gently turned my face round and our eyes met. I could no longer resist and melted into his arms, his lips seeking mine in a long lingering kiss, I found myself responding with a passion that wiped all other thoughts from my head. If there had been any doubt about how I'd felt previously then that doubt had vanished. He whispered against my ear, 'I love you.' Then, sitting back he said quietly, 'I tried not to show you how I felt. I deliberately stayed out of the way to give you time to decide how you really felt about Jim. I felt you must have feelings for me after that other evening but I couldn't be sure. It

One Life

was agony seeing you and not knowing if you really cared about me and whether you would do anything about your engagement.'

Looking into his eyes I said breathlessly, 'I love you. I knew I couldn't marry Jim after the feelings you aroused in me that evening.'

We sat quietly for a while, his arm around me and my head on his shoulder, savouring the closeness, and relaxing in each other's company. We had no thoughts for the past or future. We were enjoying our love.

Then there came the sounds of faint stirrings and the beginnings of a cry from Jennifer. She obviously wanted attention and this broke our own special magic spell. We fed her and gently settled her for the night.

'See you have both got on well together,' Sergeant O'Sullivan said, when the two of them returned from their night out. He had a twinkle in his eye and a grin on his face and added. 'I'm glad my little ruse worked,' as we left.

Peter and I talked about our future as we walked back.

'We shall have to be careful. We don't want you posted again,' he said. 'Our colleagues in the team will be OK. We will just have to find a way to get off camp and not be seen together.'

Then we kissed and said goodnight some distance from my billet so as to make sure no one saw us.

Crossing to the sick quarters next morning I was gloriously happy. The sun was burning off the early morning mist and the birds were singing. I signed in and collected the long sick list. It must be dishy blue-eyes on duty I thought. Sure enough it was, and he made sure that he was not left alone with any adoring WAAF as we worked our way steadily through the list. I was waiting for him to finish writing up the last notes before handing them to me for filing when, and to my great surprise, he said, 'I

St Eval

understand that you've broken off your engagement,' and, before I could answer, he added, 'Perhaps you would come out with me tomorrow for a meal. My name, by the way, and just for you, is Adrian.'

I was speechless and just stood there looking into those mischievous blue eyes. A long time seemed to pass and then, looking at this gorgeous man that had just paid me such a compliment, I said, 'You're having me on.'

'What makes you think that?' he said, getting up and coming towards me, 'You are free now aren't you? I've not got it wrong have I?'

'No... Yes...' I stammered. 'I mean, I am going out with someone, but it's not Jim, my ex-fiancé.

'Oh! Too late am I? Surely you can't be that serious about this new man already. I only asked you out for an evening.'

'I would have liked nothing better than to go out with you,' I replied, 'but I already have a date.'

'Ah well, I should have been quicker of the mark, do I know him?

'Yes,' I said, leaving hurriedly.

As I left I thought, here I am, in a position that any girl on the camp would love to be in, and I've turned him down.

Cornwall in summer is one of the most beautiful places to be. The landscape is stunning for as far as the eye can see. At every opportunity Peter and I would get off camp together, leaving in the ambulance so that no-one saw us.

We walked along the cliff tops and our favourite place was Bedruthan steps. The view across the famous wave-swept stacks is awesome when the tide is coming in. When the tide was out we would scramble down the damp rock stairway to the beach, take off our shoes, and paddle in the sun dappled waves rippling along

One Life

Peter and me on the right with team members, and me on the cliff tops.

the shoreline. These were wonderful, heady days. We talked together, laughed together and just basked in the sun. Sometimes we would walk hand in hand through Redruth and Truro, mingling with the holiday makers.

I lived happily from day to day but I knew this could not go on forever. Someone would find out and again I'd be posted. The team was wonderful in helping us to keep our courtship secret. Then Peter had to go away on a six weeks course and he asked the other lads in the team to look after me whilst he was away. They certainly did, taking me out swimming and sunbathing whenever our duties permitted. I had great fun with all these men, the time flew by, and soon Peter arrived back and thanked them all for looking after me.

Asian flu hit the camp and we were soon all working long duties trying to cope with the full wards. However, things gradually improved and once again I was able to snatch some time off with Peter. One day we found a sheltered cliff top outcrop

St Eval

and stretched out in the warm sunshine. I was exhausted and the sounds of the sea and the gulls soon lulled me off to sleep. I was awakened by Peter brushing my cheek gently with his lips.

'I've been sitting here watching you sleep,' he said gently, as I stretched dreamily,

'I missed you so much when I was away. 'Let's get married before either of us gets posted or separated again. Will you marry me?'

Sitting in the sun on the cliff top outcrop.

'Yes,' I said throwing all caution to the winds.

'We should get some leave sharpish then,' he said. 'You can meet my parents. We'll need permission to get married as we are both under twenty-one. What about getting you sorted first, on a weekend pass, and then we'll get leave to go to Yorkshire and get my parents' consent.'

My head began to whirl. I'd been here before and the last time I saw my mother I was engaged to Jim. Now, however, I was eighteen and no longer a ward of court. I explained this to Peter but he took over and said, 'Look, getting hold of Mrs. Edwards could be difficult, let's try your mother first.'

And on the very next weekend off we did.

We need not have worried. My mother did not even notice that Peter was not the same person I had taken to meet her before and appeared more relaxed on this visit. When asked for her signature to my marriage she simply she said she thought I was daft, and signed.

I then took him round to meet Mum and Dad Foster. They expressed surprise at the quick change in boyfriends but were as

109

One Life

hospitable as always and made Peter welcome. They said they would act in place of my parents when I did get married.

Then we returned to camp, only to find a posting for me to RAF Uxbridge hospital for continuation of my nurse training. This was to be followed, in October, by a posting to Germany. I was stunned, though I would have thought it all wonderful news had I not met Peter! I was to leave for RAF Uxbridge, a suburb of London, the following Friday. For me, just then, Uxbridge was about as far across England as you could get from Cornwall.

Before leaving I agreed to meet Peter's parents and said I would put in for a fortnights leave as soon as I arrived at Uxbridge. We had a goodbye evening with the team and Peter saw me off on my train for the journey to Uxbridge.

So much had happened in so short a time! I had progressed from 'square bashing' at Wilmslow, undergone medical training at Warton, been stationed at RAF Mount Batten, become engaged to Jim, been posted to St Eval, met a new man and broken off my engagement. And now, re-engaged, I was off again to another posting, a hospital this time, doing what I had always planned to do, and just a tube ride from London.

True I had mixed feelings, but life was certainly was not dull.

Just what lay ahead for me? I wondered.

Chapter Ten

Uxbridge

RAF Uxbridge: so there I was back in London! It was 1955. Now I could get on a tube train and visit my adoptive family, the Fosters, to plan for my forthcoming wedding.

But first, I was going to Yorkshire to meet Peter's parents. I'd been given a fortnight's leave and, though a bit apprehensive, the excitement of seeing Peter again was overcoming my anxiety.

The Foster's talked about Yorkshire people as if they were foreigners, saying, 'South is south and north is north, and never the twain should meet.'

This wasn't the last time I heard this statement. Later I found there were dialect difficulties on both sides and that they laughed at different things too.

Peter had been posted to RAF Warton, Lancashire. This happened soon after I left for Uxbridge and so he travelled to his parents a couple of days before me. I caught the non-stop overnight express to Forster Square Station, Bradford and arrived at 7 a.m. Peter and his father had overslept! Rushing to meet me, they arrived on the platform just as I was about to go through the gate.

It was ever so funny. Sticking out from the bottom of Peter's dad's trousers were his pyjamas! He was a tall, fair skinned man with mischievous blue eyes – and from what I could see, his eyes were about as much as Peter has inherited as far as physical looks went.

I was bundled into the front cab of a green Jowett van and we

One Life

set off for Peter's parent's house. Bradford was a dark, brooding, dirty looking city with tall black chimneys and dingy streets. After fifteen very bumpy minutes we turned into a cobbled backstreet. We arrived, and went in through the back door and into a warm cosy kitchen.

Peter's mum was knee high to a grasshopper, and there were traces of grey in her black hair. She was peering out at me from behind horn-rimmed glasses with her dark brown brooding eyes and there was a haughty 'better than others' air about her. It turned out that she was born into a good family in Stratford upon Avon and had enjoyed playing the violin in an orchestra. She only gave this up when Peter's father developed diabetes. Peter had obviously inherited his dark hair and colouring from her.

She was standing by a cupboard which had a sink in it and, wiping her hands on her pinny, she came over and gave me a hug, though it felt a little artificial. Then I was invited to sit down by a black range. The door was open and the coals gave off a warm glow, and I was given a cup of tea.

As soon as I could, I asked to use the toilet, as I needed to freshen up. To my astonishment, I was shown to an outhouse at the end of the yard. Entering this dark hole I saw there was a bunch of square newspaper cuttings hanging by a string from a nail on the wall. Where was the sink for washing my hands, I wondered? I soon learned that getting washed there was no private affair: we all used the sink in the kitchen cupboard and that was that.

When we sat down to breakfast, Peter's mum called and Peter's brother David came down from upstairs, but Grandma was left to sleep in for a bit. David was fifteen and took after his father. He was the opposite in colouring and height to Peter: tall, fair skinned, and with blonde tightly curled hair. He was shy and

Uxbridge

quiet and we got on well together. Although Peter's mum was friendly towards me, I felt under scrutiny, as I suppose any prospective girl friend would have done, especially one like me from down south. Peter's dad had a thick Yorkshire accent, as had his brother, and I couldn't understand what they said, but his mother's accent was as pure as cut-glass.

After breakfast Peter took me into town. It would be my birthday in a couple of weeks and he wanted to get my present. Glad to be alone together at last, we wandered around the shops, holding hands.

Peter stopped in front of a jeweller's, pointed out a gold ring with a small leaf shape of tiny diamonds, and said, 'Would you like that for your birthday present?'

My heart leapt, and, before I could answer, he had guided me into the shop. The sales girl brought the ring out of the window and I tried it on. As if by fate it fitted exactly.

Peter said, 'We'll take it.'

Then he took me to Peel Park. Entering through the gates, an expanse of green undulating grass opened up before us. Voices and laughter could be heard coming from the boats out on the lake and birds were chirping in the trees. We walked on, and under an old oak tree with dappled sunlight twinkling through the branches above, Peter took my hand and pulled me down to sit beside him. Then, taking out the ring, he took my left hand in his and again asked, 'Will you marry me?'

'Yes.'

I'd answered without hesitation and looked into his serious blue eyes as he slipped the ring onto my finger.

'I can't afford to give you a ring like Jim gave you,' he added hastily.

Looking at the ring, and then at Peter with his easy charm and

One Life

gentle ways, I replied, 'This is beautiful. I love it. I chose you. I love you,' and we embraced, oblivious of anyone else in that moment.

Eventually he said, 'I must tell my parents today. It is going to be a shock for them. I can't let you go to Germany. We must get married as soon as we can.'

Things were moving fast for me. I hadn't even been here in Bradford for more than a few hours. I felt very nervous about his parent's reaction.

That first meal with the Sugden's was a memorable occasion. Peter's grandma was setting the table with a cold meat salad. She was a wizened, frail, white-haired old woman and had a hearing-aid in her ear. This had a wire leading to a square box attached to her waist, but seemed to do little for her hearing. She spent most of her time in a chair by the fire, knitting. Peter's mother would pull back a number of rows when Grandma had gone up to bed to save wool; she said Grandma didn't know what she was knitting anyway. Grandma rarely spoke, probably because no one took the time to try to have a conversation with her, and the hearing-aid whistled incessantly. Peter's mum would reach around Grandma's waist to switch the hearing-aid off.

Grandma looked up at me with interest as we were ushered to sit down and said a hurried 'hello' then looked down again, expectantly, at her plate. Peter's dad, a diabetic, had been given his injection and now he needed to eat his meal within fifteen minutes. Routines were a big part of Peter's family life. His mum put meat first onto his dad's, and then his grandma's plate. Then she asked if we had enjoyed ourselves. Peter replied excitedly, 'We certainly have.'

Then he said he had an announcement to make, 'Margaret and I are engaged.'

Uxbridge

His mum looked stunned, but collected herself, replying tersely, 'Well, Peter, you certainly know how to drop a surprise on us.'

His father, looking first at Peter, and then searchingly at me, said quietly that he was happy for both of us. Peter went on to explain about my posting to Germany in October and said that he could not let me go. Grandma perked up, looking straight at me, and pronounced, 'She's OK. She's a southerner like me. Good for him.'

And then her head went back down and she carried on with her meal.

I warmed towards this grandma of Peter's. I had found an ally.

Discussion about life in the services and the rules on married women having to leave the services went on whilst we got on with the meal. I asked David to pass the salad cream. I took it, shook it, the lid flew off, and I covered grandma in salad cream. The family dog, a large grey haired, bear-like mongrel, seized his opportunity and proceeded to jump up onto Grandma, licking at the spilled salad cream. David collapsed in peals of laughter, and chaos ensued. This then was my first introduction to the Sugden family. Happily, the incident with the salad cream did not affect my relationship with Grandma or, indeed, the rest of the family. In fact, it broke the ice somewhat.

During the next two weeks I was taken out to see the surrounding countryside. We travelled in a black Austin belonging to Leonard who was a very close friend of the family. Leonard had lost both legs in the war when he'd trodden on a land mine. Often, his housekeeper, Mrs. Marsden, joined us.

Within fifteen minutes drive from Peter's house were the beautiful rugged Yorkshire Dales; the moors were covered with mile after mile of purple heather. We visited Haworth, the Brontë

One Life

birthplace, parks and art galleries, and the Cow and Calf rocks; these last are two huge rocks, which we had great fun climbing. Then there was Saltaire, Shipley, a fascinating place – so full of the Yorkshire mill people's history.

I fell in love with the sweeping moors and places such as Top Withens, used as a location in Emily Brontë's *Wuthering Heights*, fired my imagination, but it was difficult for Peter and I to get time off on our own. Even so, sharing this magic time with him and his family was a wonderful experience, and, like all young lovers, we found ways of escaping to be alone together.

I liked Peter's parents and, once they got over the shock of our engagement, tentative plans for the wedding were made. My posting to Germany was due to take place on October 24th and so the wedding day would have to be before this date in order to enable my discharge from the service to take place. Thus there were only two months left to plan the wedding. By that time I would only have known Peter for six months.

I explained that the Fosters were my unofficial adopted family without going into too to much detail at this stage. I was terrified that my mother would cause a scene at the wedding and even might try to stop it from going ahead. Vivid memories of Betty's wedding cake flying out of the window had left a lasting impression on my mind, together with how my mother had always tried to wreck my plans for doing anything that she had known I really wanted to do. I decided not to let her know where and when I was getting married.

Peter's parents wanted the wedding to be from their house and to take place at the family church where he and his brother were servers. We visited the vicar and he gladly agreed to marry us on the 22nd October, the bans to be called from three parishes. Then we returned to our camps and Peter and his dad looked for a flat

Uxbridge

for us in St Anne's.

I was back at RAF Uxbridge at the hospital working on shifts. I spent off duty time with the Foster's arranging their part in the wedding plans. Pop Foster agreed to give me away. There were to be four bridesmaids and Uncle George drove us all down in his Silver Cloud and put everyone who had need into a hotel for the night.

I had an interview with the Personnel Officer at Uxbridge, gave him the consent slip my mother had signed, and went through the demob process. I had always put my ambition to be a nurse before anything else, but I knew that, now I was about to become a service wife, his career would always come first.

As promised, Uncle George picked us up promptly from the Fosters for the long drive to Yorkshire. On arriving at Peter's house, we were welcomed warmly. I was to stay there overnight whilst, Peter stayed with his childhood friend and best man Robin, and the Fosters would stay in a hotel.

Excited at seeing Peter, I took little notice of the arrangements going on around me and eventually Peter and I slipped away unnoticed in the wedding chaos.

'Come on,' Peter said, 'We're off to my stag night.'

I laughed: 'You can't take me to your stag night.'

'Oh yes I can. We're going to the Midland Hotel,' he replied.

Robin, who was studying sociology at university, and Liz, his girl friend, were waiting for us. We had a good evening with them both. Despite their long time friendship Peter and Robin were as different as chalk and cheese and Robin, an outgoing lively and confident person, with blonde good looks, was following a very different career. Nevertheless they remained good friends and the evening was a lot of fun. Time flew past until Peter spotted that it was nearly midnight and we hurried to

One Life

his parent's house. They were looking everywhere for me, thinking I had disappeared.

'You can't have gone on a stag night,' they all chorused together.

'Well, she just did,' Peter laughed.

'You just get yourself to Robins. It's nearly midnight,' his mother retorted. 'Come on young lady, off to bed with you, your family were all settled ages ago.'

I went off to bed very happy.

My wedding day dawned bright and sunny. Peter's mum said, 'Happy the bride the sun shines on.'

Dad Foster proudly walked me down the long aisle of St Chad's. The church was packed and it felt dreamlike as the music of Mendelssohn's 'Wedding March' resounded around the church. As I glided down the aisle, not even the loose wooden tile that I had been warned about could trouble me. Peter had sent a message over by his best man telling me how much he loved me, written on toilet paper; it was all he could find at the time.

The marriage service progressed with the vicar saying, 'If anyone knows of any just cause or impediment as to why these two should not be joined together in holy matrimony let them now declare it or forever hold their peace.'

I came down to earth as a deathly silence descended for what seemed an eternity and then, to my great relief, the words, 'Those that have been joined together let no man put asunder,' boomed out.

Next came signing of the register, the vicar making several alterations because of the muddle over my two surnames, leaving the certificate looking just like the patchwork quilt my earlier life had been. I was at last losing the surnames – LeCorney, my mother's married name by which I had been known all my life,

Uxbridge

Wedding group with Bridesmaids, best man Robin, Peter, me and Dad Foster outside of St Chad's church.

and Ralph, my mother's maiden name which appeared on my birth certificates, in exchange for my husband's surname. Now I was a married woman and this man beside me was my husband for life and I was glad to take his name.

The reception was held in the church hall which Peter's family had decorated, and there were long trestle tables seating at least forty.

Sylvia's fiancé, a cook in the army, had made a three-tier wedding cake with a medical badge on for us. It was beautiful. A dance was to be held in the hall in the evening and I thought how lucky I was to have so many of

Me with Sylvia, my best friend and head bridesmaid.

119

One Life

Peter's family there, together with my adoptive family, the Fosters. A wistful sadness crept over me concerning my own missing relatives, but I soon shook it off and threw myself into the festivities which began with Peter and me, eyes only for each other, dancing the first waltz. After it, we left and caught the train to St Anne's where Peter and his dad had prepared our flat. As it happened, the Blackpool illuminations were on during this special fortnight that we were to spend in our new home together.

We loved Blackpool with its famous tower, the Golden Mile and its large fun fair. My nursing training had started at RAF Warton and it was here that I had celebrated my success on my eighteenth birthday. Now here I was again, having taken my discharge to get married, and on my honeymoon with my new husband. We were to live in a flat near the sea front at St Anne's until we qualified for quarters on the camp.

The flat was several flights of stairs up at the very top of an old Victorian building; the rooms were large and old fashioned, and there was a large open fire at one end of the main front room. We had to cosy up close to keep warm. We'd been given a battery wireless as a wedding present; this was our only luxury item. However we were happy newlyweds engrossed in each other; what more could we want?'

In the bedroom there was a huge old-fashioned bed with a flock mattress that you sank down into and which surrounded you in cosy warmth, and a wonderful view of the sea from an arched picture window. Awakening to the sound of the sea in the morning what more could we want? We had love, sea, and...well it was October!

And then, when we did go out, it was to feel the sea's spray amidst the dunes, screw up our eyes against the low wintry sun filtering between the scudding clouds, and watch the waves

Uxbridge

pounding the beach, their icy tendrils withdrawing, clinging, dragging, as if hungry to rip away the very shoreline and drag it down into their unfathomable depths.

What need had we of summer weather?

And in the early evening we could see from our flat the glory of an evening sunset, or the inky blackness of one of Vulcan's thunderous moods. Then, seagulls would screech as lightening seared the sky. But, whatever its mood, the sound of the sea has ever since brought back loving memories, and calmness and peacefulness to me.

My life since leaving home on that awful day had been happy and exciting. I'd met so many people, so very many good people, and, although my childhood would undoubtedly have some effects on my future. There was also so much I'd learned from my bad experiences that I knew I'd be able to put to such good use in the years ahead.

One Life

Chapter Eleven

Blackpool 1955

October and November rushed quickly past. Peter went back to work at RAF Warton camp and I found a job as a copy typist with Leyland Paints and Varnishes which was a couple of train stops down the line at Preston. Peter would, in the future, be posted to various camps in the UK and abroad. His career would come first; my career in nursing had to be put on hold. A wife accompanying her husband abroad was not allowed to work, although I was to do a good deal of voluntary work, and thoroughly enjoyed this. I had not realised how much this would help in my own career when it restarted much later in my life.

I loved our first home together. We baked potatoes and made toast on a toasting fork in front of the fire. There was a gas meter fixed outside our flat door on the landing. This had to be fed liberally with shilling pieces – hard come by on a small wage of £7.10s a week. Out of this, the rent, bus fares and food had to be paid. When cooking a cake, the meter needed feeding 1s 6p, the landlord regulating the charges and making more money. Our battery wireless was a real luxury and, of course, we were happy newlyweds, each engrossed in the other. A friendly lodger in the guise of a small mouse would come out in the moonlight and swing on the cable of our lamp by the bed. I lost all my fear of mice, watching his antics.

A friendly RAF doctor and his wife lived on the ground floor and an old lady lived in the flat below us. She struggled daily up

One Life

the stairs with her scuttle of coal. Peter told her to leave the scuttle outside her door. He would take it down and fill it, bringing it back up on his return from work. Not long after this, we found a little dish of rice pudding outside our door and sometimes a cake would appear, which was her way of saying thank you, and much appreciated by us.

Our favourite wedding present came from Peter's mum's neighbours. They all had a whip-round and gave us a mixing bowl, all the basic kitchen condiments such as salt, pepper and mustard, and many other items needed for general cooking. These included a teacloth, dishcloth and rolling pin. What a brilliant and useful present this proved to be! And, the one I remember above all the other, probably more expensive, items.

One incident in particular made me realise what a lot we had to learn about each other; we had, after all, only known each other six months on the day we got married. Peter came in from work one evening, and handed me a present, a large tin of crab. 'We can have this for tea with salad tomorrow,' he said. I hated crab, but managed to look pleased. He'd walked home from work, about seven miles each day, to save the cash to buy this treat. I managed to eat some of the crab. It would be many years later before I found I really enjoyed crab.

We had promised to go to Peter's parent's home in Bradford for our first Christmas together. It was fun shopping for presents even though we had little money to spend. I made cards, embroidered hankies and tray cloth's, and initialled a couple of hand towels.

On Christmas Eve a white blanket of snow cast its winter magic as we left the house to go to Midnight Mass. Although I had not been confirmed, Peter's mother insisted I go with them to the altar rail.

Blackpool 1955

'Keep your head bent and your hands behind your back and then the father will know you are not confirmed and bless you,' she instructed. St Chad's was High Church of England and very near to Roman Catholic in the manner of its ceremonies. The smell of the burning incense took some getting used to, especially when a server came down the aisle swinging it around at the end of a long chain. A family Christmas was a new experience for me – especially getting and receiving presents.

My sense of optimism, and my ability to see the humorous side of life, had seen me through many difficult times in my earlier childhood. However, this ability to see the funny side of most situations would not always be appreciated. I found that despite the differences between my sense of humour, and that of the Yorkshire people, Peter's brother David and I shared a sense of fun that would sometimes get us both in trouble. David had a steady low rumble of a laugh that, once it got going, would erupt into an infectious roar of laughter. On Christmas Day, attending yet another church service, we both landed in the dog house.

Leonard, a long standing friend of the family, was also a regular attendant at church services. Leonard had lost both his legs when he'd stepped on a land mine during the war. The stumps of both legs were too short for him to be fitted with artificial legs, so he got around in a wheel chair and an adapted car. There were no powered wheel chairs or ramps in those days. He lived alone, apart from his housekeeper, Mrs. Marsden, and so relied very much upon Peter's mum and dad's long term friendship.

On this particular cold, blustery Christmas Day there had been a heavy fall of snow with drifts forming by the church door. Peter's dad was helping Leonard out of the car and into the church by humping him up onto his back, Leonard's hands

One Life

From left Peter's Mother, Leonard, David (Peter's brother) and the family dog.

locked around his neck. Both of them were irritable, and grumbling at each other, as they were often wont to do. Then, as they struggled along the icy path to the church, Leonard shouted, 'I'm slipping you fool, watch out I'm slipping,' and then, suddenly, with a great plop, he lost his grip and landed in the snow drift by the door with only his head and shoulders above the snow. David put his hand to his mouth, helpless with laughter at the sight of a very indignant Leonard, and there was an astonished Dad Sugden looking down at him. This set me off and we both beat a hasty retreat round the corner of the church, trying, unsuccessfully, to control our laughter. The more we tried to calm down the more we set each other of again. It was some time before we managed, sheepishly and shamefaced, to creep into the back of the church, having regained control of ourselves.

Blackpool 1955

Later we had to apologise profusely to both Leonard and Peter's family.

All too soon, it was time for us to return to our flat after a very enjoyable Christmas.

Winter gradually turned into spring. We joined the local church and I was encouraged to take part in a confirmation class. This time I felt more ready, and was confirmed.

My friend Sylvia got married and Peter and I went down for the weekend. It was good to see the Foster's again, especially on such a happy occasion. Sylvia lived in a wooden chalet in Marlow, and soon had her first baby. Stan, her husband, left the army after a longish spell and used his discharge grant as a deposit when they decided to build their own house on the same site as the chalet.

One spring morning I felt sick on getting up. This sickness had become a feature of my mornings and, to both Peter's and my delight, my pregnancy was confirmed by the local doctor. It was now April, and, having been married for six months, we now qualified for a quarter. The rent would be deducted from Peter's pay and it would be much less than our present rent. There would also be no bus fares to find. I was sorry to leave the flat, whilst at the same time happy and excited to be moving onto the camp and into my first married quarter. This was just one of many houses and flats that we would live in over the coming years. This first married quarter was a two bedroom modern terrace house. It was fully equipped, even down to there being dusters provided, and there was a large garden at the back. The furniture was modern and solid. I was delighted. After all, how many other people then got a fully equipped home like this so soon after marriage with low rent and an allowance for coal? What a start to our wedded life!

One Life

Peter's parents were thrilled about my pregnancy. His dad was hoping for a girl as there had not been a girl in his family for generations. Peter's grandma had never ever allowed anyone to use her sewing machine, but she said I must borrow it. I enjoyed and revelled in this preparation for Peter's and my baby. I would love and cherish him or her. This baby would have all the love I had never had.

We had just managed to settle into our new home when Paul was born at the local cottage hospital. To me, of course, he was the most beautiful baby in the world with his mop of dark hair. Peter even sent me his own hand drawn card for the event – to every one's amusement on the maternity ward.

One incident stands out in my mind. A young girl was brought in the next day. She had just had her baby and was crying and distraught. She blurted out hysterically that her baby was black and that her husband had walked out of the hospital rejecting both her and the baby. She was inconsolable and in total shock. In tears she asked how she could possibly have had a black baby. She whimpered that she didn't want it and that she wouldn't see or feed it. She was blond with blue eyes and so was her husband.

'Have you a relative who is black,' I asked.

'No,' she sobbed'

'Look,' I said, 'just calm down. There must be an explanation somewhere. Have you seen anyone to talk to about it?'

'Someone is coming to see me tomorrow,' she said.

Later I went to look at the poor little scrap in his cot. He certainly was black with a head full of tight curls. He was crying for a feed and a nurse came over to give him a bottle.

'Come on gorgeous,' she said, picking him up and giving him a cuddle.

On the way back I stopped by his mum's bed to tell her what a

Blackpool 1955

lovely baby she had. She turned her face into her pillow and so I carried on to my bed and fed Paul. I was having my own feeding problems and the matron, a matriarch if I ever saw one, was giving me grief and insisting I keep trying.

After being in for five days, I was due to go home the next morning. Janet, the young woman with the black baby, had still not had a visit from her husband and was very unhappy. Peter's parents had travelled over from Bradford to stay a couple of days and visited me. I noticed then that Janet had a visitor, a young man with a bunch of flowers, and that he was very good looking. She burst into tears on seeing him and he pulled the curtains around the bed. Mum and Dad Sugden were enthralled with their grandson and looking forward to my bringing him home the next day.

After the visitors left, Janet looked more relaxed and happier and said that her husband had done some digging into his past relative's backgrounds and found out that his great-great-grandfather was black. No-one in the family had ever mentioned this fact. He was, he said, very sorry about his reaction. It had all been such a shock. Even so, and despite encouragement from the nurses and me, she still could not bring herself to go and see her baby. I don't know what eventually happened because I was discharged the next morning. I like to think she and her husband did respond to their baby and love him.

I soon settled in with baby Paul. He was a very happy and content baby and was soon sleeping through the nights.

I joined a couple of coffee mornings before Paul was born, but found these dull, I never enjoyed the coffee morning set and their trivial conversation. I tried out the keep fit mornings, and I enjoyed these, but most of the others were much older than me. They even patted me on the head to encourage me! There was a

One Life

good corporal's club on the camp and a dance was coming up. We had not been on the camp long enough to form any real friendships and we needed a baby sitter. No way did I want to leave my baby.

Peter talked to a girl in his office. She was to be cloakroom attendant at the dance with another girl.

'Why not bring baby with you?' she said. 'We will look after him. The cloakroom is large and airy and there will be two of us to keep an eye on him. It's not as though you will be far away.' So we took baby Paul with us and had a great time. We kept popping in and always found the two girls making a great fuss of him.

Peter's grandma died in the December only four months after Paul was born. I was sorry that I wouldn't have her as an ally anymore. Mum and Dad Foster visited and fussed over Paul. Winter soon turned into spring again.

Then David, Peter's brother, developed yellow jaundice. He was really poorly. When he recovered sufficiently, we suggested he come to us to recuperate, saying that the sea air would do him good. He was just 16 years old. There was a five year gap between Peter and David and consequently they had never been close. He became very much like the kid brother I'd never had.

We were talked into buying a set of encyclopaedias 'for baby Paul's future' by a very persuasive door to door salesman whilst Peter was at work. We were both worried about what he would say, as he and I could ill afford the payments. As expected Peter was not amused. It took some time to get them cancelled and collected. David stayed for six weeks. He looked much better and the yellow hue to his skin had completely gone. Peter's parents came in their Jowett van to collect David and stayed for a few days before going back home. It was now well into May. The

Blackpool 1955

weather had been kind to us. Paul was just nine months old.

I was now settled with my little family and felt safe and more confident. I hoped that one day my mother would want to be part of my life. I wrote telling her that I was married but she didn't reply. I wrote again inviting her to visit and see her first grandson. I still hoped that she could somehow come to care about me as a daughter. Peter was not happy about this. Not surprisingly he had taken an instant dislike to my mother but said that, if that was what I really wanted, then he would put up with her for my sake. Eventually, she wrote to say she was coming. As things turned out she was due to arrive on the same day that Peter's parents were due to leave. When Peter's mother realised this she was determined to delay her departure; she could not understand why I kept on trying to form a relationship with my mother after what my mother had done to me.

The visit turned out to be fraught with anxiety, although looking back it would have made a good comedy sketch. And quite amusing to watch! Two women being so polite whilst at the same time locked in an underlying and unspoken verbal combat. Peter's mother had a pious church background, and a 'holier than thou' attitude, and her conversation and attitude became more and more affected – her little finger crooked as she picked up her tea cup.

And then there was my mother with her caustic, sarcastic remarks. She never lowered her voice and could always be heard by everyone around. This caused a great deal of embarrassment for Peter and me throughout her visit. My mother had travelled from London overnight and arrived in a taxi from the station at 11.30 a.m. Even as I introduced her to Peter's parents I was alarmed by their polite yet caustic conversation.

I felt I'd better get on with getting lunch ready and then,

One Life

hopefully, Peter's parents would soon be on their way home. I made a salad and then looked in the cupboard for a tin of pineapple chunks. I found the tin just as my mother appeared at my side. Looking over my shoulder she said loudly, 'Don't bring the pineapple chunks out – we'll have those when they've gone!'

Peter's mother heard this and never forgot it. She brought it up on many occasions. I did put them out, but Peter's mother refused to have any. She didn't say anything – just the look on her face was enough! This went on until Peter's parents departed. Peter and I were just relieved that it had not erupted into an all-out battle between them. As I've said it would have made a very good comedy act if it had not been so fraught with tension for us.

My mother's stay was full of embarrassing incidents and I came to wish I had never invited her. She did her level best, whether intentionally or not, to ruin my marriage and my reputation in the neighbourhood.

'I see you have bleeding niggers,' she said, when we were on a bus to St Anne's and a black colleague of Peter's alighted and sat a few seats in front of us. We soon decided not to take her to the Corporals' mess as we had done with Peter's parents. We had black friends and colleagues who would be present. Indeed we had many friends from different cultures whilst in the forces and never came across such bigotry and prejudice as that shown by my mother. And she'd even wander down the garden path in her see-through nightie in the morning with her cup of tea – much to our embarrassment.

However, she surpassed herself on the night before she went home. Peter had gone to bed, and she'd gone to bed not long after, but, thankful for a few quiet moments on my own, I'd stayed down to tidy and put things away. I'd just sat down with a cup of tea when Peter came downstairs looking dazed and as

Blackpool 1955

white a sheet. Evidently my mother had walked into our bedroom stark naked. Thinking it was me coming to bed he had turned over and there she was – standing by the bed. Shocked he had told her, tight-lipped, to get out. The situation struck me as bizarre and somewhat funny and whether this was shock I just don't know. Peter said angrily that she had to go and I agreed.

'She is going tomorrow anyway,' I said quietly. He recovered his composure. I made him a drink, and we went to bed. My mother duly left the next morning by taxi for her train. Not a word was said about the incident. Needless to say, we never invited her to stay again.

We decided to have Paul christened at St Chad's. This was the church where Peter's parents had been married, where their children were christened, and where Peter's mother was now a Sunday school teacher. For Godparents we chose Leonard, Peter's brother David, and David's girlfriend Joan. Peter's family's life revolved around the church which I later realised was the single most important thing in their lives.

Life settled back to normal. Peter had by now signed on for a further long term in the service in order to make it his full time career and transferred into the Health and Hygiene Branch. He attended a senior trade management course to enable him to gain the rank of Sergeant. He was then transferred to the RAF Institute of Health and Medical training at RAF Halton, where he was to start his training to become a hygienist.

My second child was due in September. Paul would be just thirteen months old when the new baby arrived. At the end of August, just after Paul's first birthday, Peter was told he was to be posted overseas to Malta in the following May – an accompanied posting.

Peter's mother and father offered to have me stay with them,

One Life

for the birth of my second child, as Peter would be away studying, and taking exams, until our posting. This seemed a good idea at the time. I was excited at the prospect of living with a proper family for the first time. So the move was made in time for my second child's birth, Andrew.

Marching in and out of married quarters became a necessary routine for me over the years and was wholly my responsibility, as were the children. Peter would leave me to go to the new posting, as was the case for all other servicemen being posted. It would then be left to me to pack large crates for storage, and the small crates that would follow on to our overseas destination. To tide us over for the first three to four months, we had to take caseloads of our possessions.

Then there would be the 'marching out of the married quarter' procedure. The rituals of marching have been long remembered, not only by me, but also by my children. They have stated they remember virtually walking on their eyebrows to avoid marking the highly polished lino. Newspaper was laid down everywhere, and we lined up the cutlery, plates dishes, cups, ashtrays and the folded tea towels; blankets, sheets and pillow cases were folded in regimental style on the mattress. Windows were cleaned and pristine curtains well hung. Gardens had to be neat and tidy and lawns mowed. The type and quality of your next quarter depended on the points awarded when you 'marched out' of your last one.

These were always harassing times. On the same day as marching out, I would have to travel across the country to the airport to fly out to join Peter with the children and all our cases. What a relief when a good march out was achieved and we could get on our way. I'd not have seen Peter for some time and would be excited at the prospect of, once again, seeing and being with

Blackpool 1955

him on our new posting.

Travelling with children never fazed me. I would go well prepared with nappies, drinks, potties, games, books and puzzles. There were often long waits at stations and airports, but I don't remember my children becoming irritable or difficult and they soon became seasoned travellers.

However on this occasion I was only going a few miles to Peter's mum and dad's in Bradford. We had little in the way of our own possessions apart from wedding presents and all the paraphernalia that a baby needs. Peter could not get a leave pass as he was on his course. My neighbour next door filled me in on what was expected. The marching out was scheduled for 11.30 a.m. as I had no pressing travel arrangements that would have necessitated an early one. Dad Sugden arrived early in his Jowett van. He took baby Paul out in the garden with him whilst I finished laying out the crockery for counting. It all went smoothly and I was complimented. This meant Peter would get a good mark against his service record. As a service wife, I always had to consider what effect my actions might have on Peter's career. Peter's Dad said he thought it was nonsense – all this fuss over a house.

So here I was travelling to Bradford for an extended stay with Peter's people. I wondered how I would fare, living with a family. I was not to know, then, the difficulties I would find, or just how my confidence in myself as a mother and person would be affected.

One Life

Chapter Twelve

My Stay in Bradford

My stay with Peter's folk's was to sow the seeds of doubt in myself as a mother and shatter some of my beliefs in marriages being perfect. Peter carried on with his exams at RAF Halton, Buckinghamshire as we awaited our first and only accompanied posting to Malta.

I was put in Mum's main front bedroom as the attic was not suitable to have a baby in. I was overwhelmed that they were giving up their bedroom – no one had ever done anything like this for me. The room was large with an open grate fire and large window.

David, Peter's brother, had just started going out with Joan who was a young woman who helped with the Sunday school that Mum Sugden ran. I observed Mum and Joan talking together, they both obviously wanted the relationship to develop. I was asked my advice, but I was not getting involved. After one broken engagement I did not feel qualified to give advice. David had little to say. They were two formidable women making plans together.

The day soon came when indignant howls heralded the arrival of Andrew, my second child, into the world. He was as blond as Paul was dark, and a pound heavier.

Having a baby at home was much better than having it in hospital. The family was all around and my first born, Paul, was able to come in and be cuddled after seeing the new baby. This had to be better than bringing the new baby home after leaving

One Life

Paul feeling out of it.

Peter's father had a small French-polishing and upholstery repair business down the road. He had been apprenticed as a young boy and was a French-polisher by trade. Peter's grandfather had also been a French-polisher, and it had been expected that Peter's father would follow in his footsteps. However, much to his parent's disproval, this was not what Peter's father had planned for himself.

He'd wanted to be an artist and had originally worked in an art studio elsewhere whilst setting up his own studio in the attic. This all had to be given up when he developed diabetes. Not long after this, all inflammable items had to be removed from attics with the onset of the Second World War.

Peter's mother's dreams had also had to be shelved with her growing family commitments and her husband's diabetes. She had played the violin in an orchestra and had several friends in

Peter's Dad's Art Studio in the attic.

My Stay in Bradford

that circle. They were both somewhat bitter about giving up these dreams.

The demand for French-polishing at that time was beginning to die out, with only a few big banks needing such skills on their woodwork. Most of the work Peter's father acquired was repairing upholstery and recovering chairs. He would often get his tie caught in the upholstery covering he was sewing on the heavy duty treadle machine. When this happened he would simply cut through his tie and leave the trapped bit inside. Health and safety meant nothing in those days. He also sold venetian blinds, carpets, braids and fittings to supplement his small income.

He delighted in winding me up by insisting that I leave baby Paul to play in his shop whilst I made my daily trips to the nearby shops for food. He allowed Paul to pull out boxes of nails, mixing them all up, and to play with his latex glue and then roll about in the flock covering the floor. Paul would look like a snow man after being in the shop. Dad, as I now called him, told me he used to deliver the repaired items on a hand cart before he had the Jowett van. He often took me and the children along with him for the ride out. The number of these trips gradually increased and he made up all sorts of excuses to Mum Sugden, as often he had no furniture to be delivered. The children and I really enjoyed these outings. The Yorkshire countryside and the moors were really beautiful and there were many interesting places to see. The trips also helped me to get used to Peter's Dad's dialect and actually understand what he was saying. When Peter's mum realised what Dad was doing she put a stop to it. Work must not be neglected, just so as we could go on these trips out, she said.

Dad Sugden had put me on a pedestal. I was the first woman

One Life

to join a family which was mostly male. I was soon to fall off with a bump. Mum was taken very much for granted. The men never fetched or carried coal from the coal house and they expected her to run about and wait on them hand and foot, cleaning their shoes and putting their slippers on for them. She had very little in the way of modern equipment. A dolly tub with corrugated scrub board sufficed for washing and a wooden mangle was kept out in the back yard under the window to wring it out. The rollers were so badly worn in the middle that there was a large gap where they should have met. I tried to ring out sheets and scrub the nappies in the antiquated dolly tub. All this took place out in the yard. It was often freezing cold and no fun at all trying to turn the handle of this monstrosity of wringer with my icily numb fingers. To add insult to injury, the bucket underneath did not always catch the squeezed-out water which would end up soaking my feet instead.

The babies had to be bathed in the kitchen sink which was hidden in a cupboard. There was no bathroom in the house and no room for a baby bath and stand to be put up in the kitchen. I had come from London where we'd had a (mostly) modern equipped flat, and even a telephone. This was proving to be a real culture shock for me!

As my life moved forward there would be many changes and I was often to experience the contrast between having luxury things abroad, with local servants to help in the house, and not having much of anything back in England. This never again fazed me. I was happy with either one scenario or the other, appreciating that, much as I enjoyed having nice things around me, kindness, caring and love were far more valuable. Both as a child and an adult money really meant little in itself, though I did enjoy the luxuries!

My Stay in Bradford

Mum Sugden also had great difficulty in getting money for food out of Dad Sugden. She would keep asking him for money, as the totals 'on tick' mounted up at the local shops, and everyone from the butcher to the baker asked for their bills to be paid. Dad could be awkward and cantankerous. Diabetes, I was told, can affect a person's temperament; however, I was also told that Dad's own father had been a cantankerous, awkward alcoholic.

I had a lot to learn about ways of approaching things and being helpful. I had been made to do chores around the house to a very high standard as a child, so one day I was washing up after a meal whilst mum Sugden went to the shops, when I decided to give the stove a thorough clean. I took it to pieces as I had often done for my mother. But, oh dear, it was certainly not appreciated! Peter's mother was not pleased at all, taking great umbrage at my efforts, and asking if her house was not clean enough for me. This was a real echo from the past and although the reaction this time was not as explosive, and violence did not ensue, I found it hard to accept the rejection of my innocent help. I saw that I had a lot to learn about handling domestic situations and that I was still an outsider to this family! I retrieved myself somewhat by apologising and assuring her this was certainly not my intention to criticise anyone. Then I unpacked the saucepans that Peter and I had been given as a wedding present and gave her them to use with her own kitchen items, and this she did appreciate.

People found it hard to understand my southern accent. I found that some similar sounding statements meant different things in different cultures. This was not to be the last time I would feel more of a foreigner in parts of my own country than I felt abroad. An episode one Friday demonstrates this. Just as Monday was cold meat day, Friday was fish day in the Sugden household, and I'd been asked to go to the fish shop for fish and chips. I duly asked for 'four fish and chips, please'. Back home, Mum opened the wrapping and there were indeed four fish but only one portion of chips.

'I did ask for four fish and chips,' I said.

Mum replied, 'Well you got four fish didn't you, just what you asked for, and one lot of chip's.

Still not understanding, I replied, 'I asked for four fish and chips.'

Again she pointed out that anyone locally would have assumed that I had asked for four fish but only one lot of chips.

'You should have asked for fish and chips four times.' she said.

I also had not heard of 'baps' and many other strange Yorkshire colloquial words.

I began to think that things were not always as they would appear and that marriage was not the end of the rainbow. Having no father, and a mother who did not want me, let alone love me, had left gaps in my knowledge of relationships. I had therefore developed in my mind a fantasy of the perfect marriage and family.

I learnt from Mum Sugden, in conversation, that she would have married Leonard, had he not lost his legs, rather than Dad, but that by doing this she felt that Leonard had withdrawn himself from the marriage mart. She also had another admirer, one Alec, who still called quite often. I could not but wonder about how strange this marriage was when, on Mum Sugden's birthday, Alec called with a card in the form of a frame with a poetic birthday wish and a bunch of flowers. I came in with a tray of tea and cakes to find them holding hands. Although not significant in itself I noticed she had moved Dad's card to the

My Stay in Bradford

side of the mantelpiece and put Alec's in the middle. When Dad came in he noticed the framed card from Alec and swapped them over, replacing his card in the middle. Mum, very pointedly, again swapped them around and, on coming back into the room, Dad again swapped them back. This went on for a couple of days. On the surface their marriage appeared to be perfect with never a cross word said in front of the children, but I could not help but wonder at just what made a real happy marriage after this incident.

I later realised that no one, including the children, could ever know what went on inside of a marriage. Sometimes one could believe a marriage was unhappy when in fact the couple actually enjoyed their arguments and a little sparring, even though this might appear to outsiders to be such odd behaviour towards one another.

Mum suffered with diverticulitis. This came and went and erupted whilst I was with them. When the doctor called he told her that in order to relieve the situation, she would need an operation to remove the part of the bowel most affected. Since I was there to look after Dad Sugden and David, she agreed to have it straight away. Little did I know how difficult both of them would become.

The operation and her recovery went well and she came home a couple of weeks after the operation. The specialist advised a short walk each day in the fresh air and said she would be fine.

However Mum went straight to bed on arriving home and would not get up, even when the doctor came to see her. He said there was no reason to stay in bed. She should be up and about and going out for short walks. She just appeared to have given up, and I, always obedient to my own mother's orders, felt unable to be firm with her.

One Life

I found life hectic with two babies as well as being at Dad's beck and call. I asked David to clean his own shoes, and bring the coal in for me, which he did happily. However Dad would not even take his sandwich with him for his morning break, determined that I should walk down with it. This, like all his meals, had to be there for him by a certain time. Everything had to be exactly on time. I did understand this. As a diabetic he had to keep to routine.

After three weeks my money ran out and the shop keeper remarked that the tick bill was mounting up so I asked Dad Sugden for some housekeeping. Over the next week he ignored my pleas. Eventually I noticed a brown packet pined high up on the wall over the fire place with some money inside. Assuming it was the housekeeping I paid off the tick at the local shop and then at the butchers.

He was not pleased that Mum would not get up. He sulked and grumbled at me, vying for attention with the children. The situation came to a head one morning when I put his breakfast in front of him after he had given himself his usual injection. I'd then poured him a cup of tea and turned round to prepare baby Andrew's bottle and Paul's breakfast, before getting them up. I could hear Paul shouting and baby Andrew was crying. Suddenly there was a thud close by. I turned round and there was Dad Sugden floundering on the floor, having allowed himself go into a diabetic hypo, not having eaten the breakfast in front of him. Rushing over, I tried to get some sweetened tea into him. He was dazed and sweaty, flailing about aggressively and pushing me away. I was aware that diabetics could become really aggressive when going into a hypo but I had never seen Dad ever be aggressive. I managed to get the tea down him with great difficulty and he pulled round, eventually sitting back in his chair

My Stay in Bradford

and sulkily eating his breakfast. I was now angry and upset, determined this could not go on. I could not cope with Dad doing this to me again. What if he went into a coma, I thought.

It had been three weeks since the doctor had seen Mum so I called him out after Dad had gone to work. I explained tearfully what had happened, and asked him to again check if Mum was alright to get up, and to tell her she must do so as I could not go on like this. He agreed with me saying that I would be ill if things went on as they were. It was all so unnecessary. She needed to be up and about for her own sake and he would tell her so.

Years later, with maturity, training and knowledge of depression I am sure I would have handled this situation much better; however, I was young, totally inexperienced, and out of my depth.

The doctor examined Mum and again told her she was fit and well and should be up and about and not leave me to cope alone. However she had still not got up when David arrived home, just as I was bathing the children ready for bed. I was distraught, not knowing what to do next, and he asked what was wrong. At this I just burst into tears, spilling out the day's events. He told me not to worry – he would speak to Mum.

I looked up in surprise for David had never stood up to his parents. In fact, on one occasion a while back, he had been sick down his shirt after drinking with his friends, and had hidden his shirt in a drawer. On finding the shirt Mum had launched into a tirade. She made him go down on his knees to her, with me present, and beg her forgiveness, promising never to get drunk again. She had humiliated him in front of me. I was appalled.

However, now he went upstairs to see his mother. What he said I do not know, but whatever it was she was down stairs the next morning. With Mum present, Dad behaved. However, I had

One Life

well and truly fallen off the pedestal where he was concerned.

Now that Mum was downstairs her friends called to see her in the afternoons. She was holding court, crooking her little finger when drinking her tea, and telling them that Peter was going to be Health Inspector for the whole island of Malta, just as I came into the room with freshly baked buns.

'Isn't he?' she said, looking at me for acknowledgment.

Irritated, I replied, 'Well, yes, if that's what you call being a rat catcher for the services.'

I hated snobbishness and I could always be counted upon to rise to the situation if provoked. Sometimes, I thought afterwards, I could do with sticking plaster across my mouth. She never forgave me for this. However I got on well with Mum on the whole. The same could not be said as far as getting on with Dad was concerned. The tension began to rise again as he undermined my authority with the children, especially at meal times. He would give Paul titbits from his plate, despite my asking him not to, and then Paul would not eat his own food.

'Nothing I say or do with my children appears to be right with you, Dad,' I said on one occasion in exasperation.

From then on Dad decided not to have any conversation with me, but he did keep up his critical remarks and, of course, I would answer back. Dad had always wanted a daughter and I was proving a disappointment. He must have been angry at this cheeky Londoner. I was not at all respectful and subservient towards the men folk as the woman of his generation were.

Paul was having accidents, after being clean for ages, probably finding he had to vie for my attention. Mum going into hospital had not helped and I had less time to do things individually with him. At the time though I felt this was because I was not doing things right. I must be a poor mother. How could

My Stay in Bradford

I be a good mother? I had not had anyone to show me. I had no role model! My self confidence was beginning to disappear more each day. I didn't need Dad's constant critical remarks.

This would not be the last time I would lose my confidence as a mother.

It all came to a head one Friday; I was giving Andrew, now a tubby eight month old, his bath in the sink and the guard was around the fire with his clean clothes on it ready. I had been used to having a baby bath for my first baby and a place to lay him down safely whilst I dried him. I lifted him out of the sink, wrapping the towel round him. I was sitting down with this wriggling, slippery baby in my lap, trying to avoid the chair arms whilst drying him, when he slipped to the hearth with a plop and an indignant howl. As I picked him up to check if he was OK, and to give him a cuddle, Dad caustically remarked that I was not fit to be a mother. I couldn't even hold on to my baby. At this something inside me snapped. Pushing Andrew at Peter's mother, I turned on my heal, and I said over my shoulder, 'Well if you're such wonderful parents you can have him!' and walked out of the house, slamming the door.

I walked and walked, ending up at St Chad's church. Inside I sat down. I was feeling an absolute failure. I sat for some time gradually calming down. It was so peaceful. I picked up a bible from the pocket at the back of the chair in front of me and opened it at random. I can't now remember what it said although I did find it comforting. I sat there for some time. The vicar eventually came in and we talked. I told him quietly what had happened, that I had lost my rag and stormed out. He listened, not condemning me, and asked how I felt now.

'Not so angry, just drained and unhappy, I don't want to go back. I just can't cope, living with Peter's people. I'm not good

147

One Life

enough for them,' I said.

'Oh come on now! None of us is perfect. God does not expect us to be. It's not easy for them, having two babies suddenly living with them. You have coped with your mother in law all through her illness, which must have been difficult. I am sure they are very worried about you.'

'If Peter was here to stand by me it would not be so bad. He should be coming home to-night'.

'Well, you can talk it over with him then,' he said.

I felt better after our talk. I had been 'hot headed'. I was still feeling very nervous at going back when who should come into the church but Peter. Leonard had been driving around looking for me at the request of the family and, not having found me, had returned to the house. Then Peter had turned up. He said he knew of one place I may be: the church. So he and Leonard had set off and now here he was. I was overjoyed to see him, thanking God quietly, and feeling I could face anything now he was with me.

Chapter Thirteen

A Posting to Malta

Malta was our first posting abroad. The year was 1958 and we were to spend two and a half years on this island. I was excited to be going abroad for the first time. Malta is situated in the middle of the Mediterranean Sea and is part of an archipelago of three islands: Malta, Gozo and the much smaller Comino.

We were greeted by sun-drenched scenery and the glistening blue waters of the Mediterranean. We stayed in a Hotel in Valetta until finding a high-standard, ground floor flat in Manamah. We were even given an allowance to have a maid. This was sheer luxury for me, having two small children, as well as providing much needed employment for local people. Rose, a lively, likeable 17 year old, who was extremely good at her job, did all the washing, ironing and housework. My time could now be devoted to my two little boys and Peter.

Paul and baby Andrew settled down quickly. They loved paddling and splashing around on the sands and in the sea, and thrived in the Mediterranean sunshine. These were happy, idyllic times and we visited the historical sights of Malta with our new found friends and their children. There was so much history to see on this small, predominantly Catholic island with some of the oldest known churches in the world.

Driving in Malta was an experience and a half; the local people tended to cross themselves and go, seemingly putting themselves in the hands of God. After experiencing these notorious local roads we came to believe they must be right. How

One Life

Eddie, Marian, Peter and me.

else could they survive their own hair rising driving? This did not, however, deter Peter from getting his first car.

We made four very different friends whilst in Malta. Marian and Eddie – they lived in the flat across the hall from us. Marian was 15 years older than me, in her forties, with one daughter of 12 years, and a second, much younger daughter the same age as my Paul, who had just had his second Birthday.

I suppose it was an odd friendship really. Marian was tall, with shoulder length dark hair, and old-fashioned ideas about children. Although kind, she felt that children should be seen and not heard. Amanda, her youngest daughter, would sit sucking her thumb, and rarely laughed. To begin with she was a very solemn, quiet child, though this changed after being with my boys for a while. She very soon became a laughing, mischievous bundle of fun.

I well remember Marian offering to have the boys one afternoon. I was not sure about this as my children could get up to real mischief if not watched closely. I usually found it best to

A Posting to Malta

down tools and join them during the holidays and even in term time I liked to do something with them after school. Nonetheless, I was tempted. It would mean I could go to the shops unfettered by the children. I found that I could not resist the opportunity.

However on arriving back, I found Paul standing in the corner with Amanda, Andrew sitting on a chair, and Marian red faced. She usually baked cakes on a Monday. She would take the butter out of the fridge, unwrap it, and put it on the ornate dining room table to soften for use in her cooking. There was a bird in a cage at the side of the table. Marian had left the children playing whilst in the kitchen. On hearing the bird shrieking, and loud giggles coming from the dining room, she walked through to find Amanda and Paul polishing the table with the butter and Andrew swinging the bird cage from side to side. Butter and bird seed was everywhere and the bird looked as though it was about to have a heart attack. I retrieved my two boys, apologised, and beat a hasty retreat. Fortunately, Marian later saw the funny side of the situation saying, 'I realise there is a big gap between my two children and it is good for Amanda to be able to be with others of her own age.'

I explained that I never let my two boys out of my sight and found it easier to let them join in with what I was doing. I found out later that one child on its own rarely got up to the mischief that two would together.

We regularly took the children to the beach. I was prepared for all contingencies, having extra pants and trousers with me, for, if distracted, one of the boys would invariably run back in the water after being dressed. Of course Amanda joined in with my children. Marian was very forbearing, and we never fell out about the children. For this I admired her. Later in life I was to experience just what it was like to be a mature mother.

Malta was to be the beginning of my travels around the world as a service wife at a time when travel abroad was yet to become available for most people. Life for me was to be very different from what was still something of the norm for most people: that is, a life spent living in just one area of England and staying with the same friends. Somehow, service friendships seem different, stronger and more lasting than those made in childhood, or when you are settled in one place.

The Air Force and the Army also appeared to be different in the way they posted personnel. The Army would post their personnel wholesale in regiments. The wives and husbands therefore had the same colleagues wherever they went. The RAF appeared to treat personnel as individuals. There were also different sections within a camp – for example: Transport, the Cookhouse, Stores, Maintenance, the Medical Centre, and so forth.

If someone was a medic by trade, he or she would be posted to the medical section on the camp. As individuals they may well find that they do not know any of the personnel in the section they are newly posted to, though sometimes they may come upon old colleagues that they have worked with before. When discovering an old friend on a posting to a new camp the friendship would often be taken up as if there had not been a break. This happened in the case of Marian and Eddie. When they vacated their flat on leaving Malta at the end of Eddie's tour of duty, we met up again with other old friends, Christine and Bill who moved into Marian and Eddie's flat.

However, losing touch could still be very easy, both with service friends and with old-established friends at home, as either could move. Postings, usually of two-and-half year's duration,

A Posting to Malta

sometimes lasted only eighteen months, or even less in the case of some of our UK postings. One could very easily lose contact with service friends, who were themselves moved regularly, so meeting up again was greeted with joy.

Christine and Bill had identical twin boys who were the same age as Paul. Christine, a petite, good natured woman in her mid-twenties, had dark short hair and hazel eyes. Her two boys, Christopher and David, both had blue eyes and blond wavy hair. Identical in every way, it was impossible for most people to tell them apart to start with, but as I got to know them I learned that, whereas Christopher was mischievous with a ready grin, David was shy and slower to relax. My sons, with just 13 months between them, were physically very different. Paul was small, with black wavy hair and blue eyes, and was a quiet, gentle natured and shy child. In contrast Andrew, thirteen months younger, was boisterous, blonde haired and sturdy, and had caught Paul up in height. The four boys soon became firm friends.

You would not have picked Bill out from a crowd, but he had a likeable personality and was fun-loving with a great sense of humour. He was an RAF photographer by trade and taught me a great deal about photography. Whilst in Malta, Peter bought our first Rolleiflex camera and Bill managed to get us an old printing and developing kit and taught me how to load the Paterson developing tank in the darkness of the wardrobe in our flat. Christine would close the door on us, and put a blanket over the crack, whilst she and Peter sat and had a drink together. We then loaded the plastic tank in the small confined space of the wardrobe. It was rather claustrophobic. Once Peter and Christine forget us and we had to shout to get their attention. We were both very hot and sweaty by the time they let us out. They just

One Life

laughed. Bill also taught me printing and developing. This photographic hobby, started at fifteen on the holiday to Jersey, was to stay with me for my lifetime.

Whenever an opportunity presented itself, our cameras would come out. There were many religious festivals in Malta and churches would be lit up, resplendent with many light bulbs adorning them and my camera would be on overdrive, clicking away.

At times Christine lacked confidence when dealing with her twins. I could understand this, having experienced this myself, and at this time I was able to support her. Strange as I, myself, was later to lose my confidence completely.

Soon after arriving in Malta we heard of a scheme where we could save, over a year, for tickets so that a relative could have a holiday of a life time with us. We started saving hard to bring Peter's mum and dad out for a holiday. We were so much enjoying being in Malta and we wanted to share some of this with them. It could be

Bill with his twins on the outside and my boys in the middle.

our way of thanking them for having me stay with them. We felt they would enjoy a stay with us, especially since they had never been abroad before. Very few people were able to afford to travel abroad at that time. What a struggle it was to save the amount of money needed! After saving for months we still only had enough

A Posting to Malta

for one full ticket and a little extra. Flights were very expensive with stops to refuel taking a long time. Peter's mum told us in a letter that his dad was going blind as a consequence of his diabetes. So she suggested that he come on his own and that she would come later, perhaps next year when we had been able to add to the fund. We agreed and booked the flight.

We were determined to give him a good time. Having a housemaid we could give more time to him and his needs. He arrived midsummer and thoroughly enjoyed himself.

We had a beach tent so that he would not be burned by the sun as he was fair skinned. He came well prepared to cope with his diabetic needs, we took him all around the island, and he went home happy after his first and only trip abroad.

Peter's Father with the boys at the catacombs and on the beach.

My third child, Jeanine, was to be born the following year. We talked to the boys about the forthcoming arrival. Paul enjoyed helping with the planning but Andrew was not too pleased and would not join in. Christmas was nearly upon us, a big event in Malta and one enjoyed by all. The weather was warm, certainly compared to British standards, and of course there wasn't any snow!

One Life

In March Jeanine introduced herself to the world at the nearby Royal Navy hospital, weighing in at six pounds. We were delighted at having a daughter and celebrations were held by us in Malta, and at home in Yorkshire by Peter's mum and dad. It was at these times that my mind would dwell on my own lack of relatives.

We decided that now our family was complete. It was wonderful not having the washing to do; we had the loveable side of this baby with none of the hard work. She was a good, content baby. All my babies had been contented – sleeping through the nights.

We had now managed to save enough for an air ticket for Peter's mum. At last she was coming out to Malta and what better time. We were determined that she would enjoy herself as much as Dad had on his first holiday abroad. She got very excited and really enjoyed the flight over.

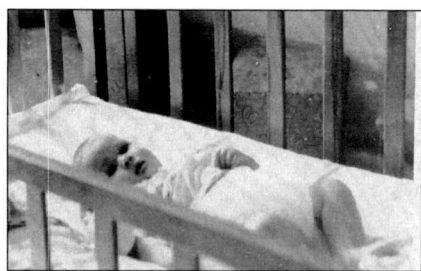

Peter's mother with my boys.   *Jeanine in her cot.*

She adored Jeanine, who was such a happy baby and giggled and laughed all the time. She hated not being in charge of things in the flat though. She seemed to feel usurped by the maid who did everything. I told her to enjoy being waited on, but she did not like the heat, the flies, Malta itself, or indeed anything about the island and she made this very clear to both of us. Older

156

A Posting to Malta

people did not always set an example, I thought, and we were very disappointed. We had gone to such trouble and saved so hard for her trip, but she was determined not to let herself enjoy the holiday!

I'd had had so little love and care as a child that every pleasant, new experience had been exciting and a thrill for me. This had taught me to really appreciate good things when they happened. Peter's mum and dad had opened up their home for me before I came to Malta and we had wanted to show them that we were grateful and loved them by bringing them out to Malta but it was a relief when she went home.

Peter just said, 'Never mind, we tried, and you can't make people enjoy them selves.' I was to realise much later that Mum's sole purpose in life appeared to be one of martyrdom. Maybe her disappointments in life had left their mark. She seemed to gain some perverse enjoyment out of being a martyr.

Soon after this a bout of measles overcame Paul, Andrew, and Jeanine who was only four months old. We were worried but pleased that, as a girl, she had got this out of the way. I had never had any of the childhood illnesses, probably because I had spent a good deal of time in hospital at such an early age and I did not appear to be catching any from the children either. We really enjoyed our stay in Malta, but it was now coming to an end. Rose, our much appreciated maid, was getting married the week before we left to return home and we were invited to the wedding. As was the local custom, the bride's new home was adorned and opened up for visitors to look around. We all sat in rows and were presented with small glasses of wine. We then queued up down the aisle to wish the bride and groom well. It was an interesting experience.

We now looked forward to returning to the UK, to a temporary home in Blackpool, and our first real cup of tea in two and a half years.

One Life

Chapter Fourteen

Blackpool RAF Transit Camp

RAF Blackpool was used for families awaiting allocation of a quarter on the camp to which the serviceman had been posted. We were housed in old, wartime tunnel-shaped Nissen huts. Each hut was divided in half and there was a door at each end leading into one main room with a kitchen and bedroom. Thus our basic needs were met.

Nissen huts have a fascinating history. They were invented by US born Colonel Peter Norman Nissen of the Royal Engineers in 1916 as housing for the troops in WWI. Their semicircular, corrugated-iron structure was found to deflect shrapnel from shell and bomb blasts and, in their unbuilt state, each one exactly filled the back of a 3 ton truck. They were the original prefabs and, like many others of these supposedly temporary buildings, many survive to this day.

As I'm sure you can imagine, returning to an English sea-side resort in November was a real change from living in comfort in Malta. Even so, and strangely enough, I never found coming home to England and readjusting difficult. Maybe it was the excitement of a new place to live and my conviction that family togetherness far outweighed anything material.

Peter had been posted to RAF Ouston. This had first been built as a fighter base, opening in March 1941, and was situated in wild and inhospitable moorland area some six miles from Newcastle. We were to join him as soon as a married quarter became available. Thankfully summer soon arrived and we had

One Life

Peter's mum and dad, and Joan and David, visit us to enjoy the fun of the seaside just before our move.

From left Peter's Dad, Mum, David, Joan and Peter.

We moved from the temporary transit camp to RAF Ouston soon after Mum and Dad's visit. The children settled in quickly and Paul started his first school. He appeared settled and happy and his teacher said he was a loquacious and delightful boy to teach. Jeanine was now running about and she soon became potty clean, not least because of the 'help' from her brothers who chased after her with the potty.

Baby sitters were in abundance amongst the WAAFs, so we were able to spend evenings in the mess. We both joined the drama group. I offered to be the prompter when the present prompter was posted. The play being put on at the NAAFI restaurant was *Sailor Beware*. Peter was playing the part of Henry Hornet, the brow beaten husband, and it was great fun.

Blackpool RAF Transit Camp

Then, disaster: on the first night the person playing Mrs Lack was taken ill and hospitalised with appendicitis.

As there was no one to fill the gap for the show that evening, I was asked if I could walk the part through with a book. Of course there would have to be an apology to the audience but, as prompter, I was familiar with most of the parts. In the event, I managed without the book! My part was that of a nosey neighbour who read the tea leaves in cups.

Me, centre table playing Mrs Lack.

The evening performance began and I donned Mrs Lack's cross over apron and headscarf. Then I put my tea cup down absent-mindedly and only remembered to snatch it out of Mrs. Hornet's way at the last minute as she sat down. This was not in the script but it brought the house down and there was much laughter at the reaction from Mrs. Hornet. We were ad libbing as we went along. All the others were delighted. They said that I

161

The signed programme.

was a dark-horse, and a natural, and we must keep the script just as we had done it that night. I never mentioned I had stage experience so as not to raise expectations of me. This was the first of many happy times, for both Peter and me, in drama groups throughout the services.

Blackpool RAF Transit Camp

Peter bought a little van and we had outings and made visits to see his mum and Dad and Peter's brother and his wife to be.

David and Joan got married later and Peter was best man. I made kilts for the boys who were to be page boys and Peter made them sporrans.

David and Joan's wedding with my boy's as page boys.

We were at Ouston just fifteen months before being posted to RAF North Weald where I would confront my life crisis.

One Life

Chapter Fifteen

RAF North Weald – A Life Crisis

North Weald turned out to be the place where I would meet my 'life crisis,' confront my past, and come to terms with who I am.

The village of North Weald was home to North Weald Airfield which played a major role in the Battle of Britain. Paul started at his new, second school just down the road. He was finding it more and more difficult to settle in each time we were posted. These moves from school to school were becoming of mounting concern to me. Andrew, a very active, loveable and mischievous child, was given to bouts of stubbornness which could erupt into outbursts of temper.

When Paul started school, Andrew, who still had a year to wait, was miserable and would sit sucking his thumb. No amount of encouragement seemed to help until we bought our first Bakelite twelve-inch TV.

There were only a couple of children's TV programs shown then. In the morning there was *Watch with Mother* or *Bill and Ben the Flower Pot Men*, and a school's programme on Shakespeare! Andrew would suck his thumb and sit there, avidly watching. He pined for his daddy who had to set off on his inspections of camps all over the country on a Monday and did not return until late Friday evening. Fortunately Jeanine was happy and content to exploring her surroundings.

I made two very good friends in Ruth and Stan. Ruth was dark-haired, of ample proportions, had a great sense of humour,

165

One Life

and was fun loving and good natured. Stan, her husband, was tall and slim and he was also good natured and easy going. One could, though, sense the sadness behind this outwardly happy couple's appearance.

The couple had two children, Mandy, and Jonathan who had hydrocephalus. Now nine years old he could not walk, talk, understand or communicate in any effective way, but he was strong, and it was difficult to cope with him. He could shuffle across the floor like lightning and would dismantle and damage household items, swiftly causing chaos around him. He also had no concept of time and place and was in need of full-time attention.

Ruth and Stan, who loved him dearly, were rapidly coming to the time when they would not be able to cope with him but they did not want to recognise this and let go. We always tried to dwell on the funny side of an incident. This could be very difficult at times. Thus on one occasion he saw a pair of red shoes and proceeded to pick them up. Unfortunately my daughter, not yet two and half years old, was wearing them and she was none too pleased at suddenly finding herself in a heap on the floor. Fortunately, she was unhurt except for her pride.

Then there was the picnic we had together. Ruth's eyes were distracted from Jonathan for a few seconds whilst the children were eating jelly and ice cream at a small table in their dormer van when suddenly Mandy's dish went flying past Ruth's ear and out through the van window. This was followed by Jeanine's. Paul and Andrew were hanging on to theirs for dear life as Jonathan's arms flailed about trying to grab them. It was complete chaos.

Occasionally I looked after Jonathan. Ruth would leave long lists of his needs and warnings on how to cope. I found these

RAF North Weald – A Life Crisis

times very exhausting, attempting to change a nappy on a nine-year-old as big as myself was a challenge.

It was no use expecting him to help by being still. He'd just carry on with whatever he was doing. He would playfully throw his arms around me, knocking all the air out of me as he clasped me in a bear-hug, and then he'd pat me on the back. Once I turned my back on him for a split second only to find him eating coal from the coal scuttle. He slept little at night and would climb out of his bed and demolish the room.

Events came to a head when Ruth became pregnant. Jonathan could reach for things and pulled furniture over at times. How would a new baby fare, never mind all the paraphernalia of carry cots, prams and the like that would come with it?

Andrew, Paul and Jonathan (right) picnicking.

Stan had a talk with me, Ruth had now been advised not to pick Jonathan up or she could lose the baby. Stan had been given names of a couple of good homes where Jonathan could be well cared for. It was hard for them to acknowledge that he did not even know them as his parents. What parent wishes to believe this?

One Life

I talked with Ruth and cared for Jonathan as often as I could to give her a break. I pointed out the dangers to the new baby and encouraged her to look at a couple of homes. We visited them and spent some time there. Ruth observed the staff and their kind, caring handling of the children. She was beginning to come to terms with the situation.

At the home Jonathan would have the freedom of a large room with no danger from furniture. He'd be able to race around on his bottom as much as he liked. Arrangements were made for him to go into the home for a short stay before Ruth had the baby and he did stay there until she and the baby were settled-in at home.

Ruth had a lovely baby boy and, after a couple of near accidents, Jonathan eventually went into the home on a permanent basis. Ruth needed much love and support at this time and my heart went out to her in her struggle to come to terms with losing Jonathan. She and Stan soon realised, after visiting him several weekends, that Jonathan did not recognise them, though he did recognise their dormer van because of its bright red colour. Eventually Ruth realised he was happy and did not miss them.

I relate this friendship in some detail as it has a bearing on the following events which were to show me just how important and precious friends, and the caring support they give to each other at times of need, are. True friends are rare and I consider myself lucky to have had true friends.

One afternoon, to my surprise, I found Bill on my doorstep. He and Christine were back from Malta and were posted to North Weald and had heard we were here too. They'd been allocated a quarter just a couple of doors down the road.

Christine arrived with the children the following week. How they'd grown since we last saw them in Malta! All the children

RAF North Weald – A Life Crisis

soon settled into their old friendship with my boy's walking to school with theirs as a foursome. Ruth, Stan, Christine and Bill got on very well. We had days out together and Ruth's dormer-van heaved with children at times as we all went on picnics.

Life was good, and I did not see the storm clouds gathering on the horizon.

Sometimes, with Peter away, I found myself sometimes wishing the week away. However much you love them, three small children to care for inevitably brings restrictions as to what one can do. I particularly felt the lack of adult conversation in the evenings which were spent very much on my own. Events were to overtake me one wet cold Friday evening. I was expecting Peter home, but I never quite knew what time he would arrive.

On this particular Friday I had a strange feeling of foreboding. It was late and Peter had still not arrived. I began to worry. We had no telephones in our houses in those days. After hours of waiting the doorbell rang. I opened the door to find one of Peter's colleagues standing there. He just said, 'Peter has had an accident. We were travelling together in my car. I got him straight to hospital.' He then pushed a plastic bag with Peter's jacket in at me saying, 'Sorry,' as he turned to leave.

I said, 'Thanks for letting me know.' Then I shut the door, as if nothing out of the ordinary had been said.

I walked through to the kitchen as if in a dream, staring straight ahead of me. I opened the plastic bag and lifted out Peter's jacket. One sleeve, and the front of it, was soaked in blood. I looked at it in shock and panic: what on earth could have happened to him? Slowly I crossed the road to Ruth and Stan's and rang their bell. Stan answered and saw me, just standing, staring straight ahead. Then he saw Peter's blood-stained jacket in one of my hands, and on the fingers of the other still on the

One Life

bell. Gently he lifted my finger off the bell and said, 'What has happened?' Ruth appeared behind him and they both put their arms around me and led me into their house. Ruth looked out behind me to see if anyone else was there and, seeing my door open, she went to check on the children before returning and then she too asked me what had happened.

'Peter's been in a car accident,' I said. 'He's in hospital.'

'Which hospital?' asked Ruth?

At this I was jogged out of my dazed state a little.

'I don't know. The chap he was travelling with just said he had taken him to the hospital, gave me his jacket, and left.'

'How could he just give her his jacket and leave her in this state?' Ruth asked Stan,

'Did he not give you any more details?' Stan asked.

'No, he just left.'

'He should have stayed with you until he got someone in to support you,' Ruth said angrily. 'He should also have made sure you knew all the facts, especially exactly what had happened to Peter, and which hospital he was in.'

Stan went to the guardroom to try and find out where Peter was and just what had happened whilst Ruth arranged with Christine to have the children.

Stan returned in the early hours of the morning, having had no luck either in finding where Peter was or what had actually happened to him. He would, he said, go to work and make enquiries through the official channels.

He eventually called in at 10 a.m. that morning. It had been difficult to find details about the accident because Peter's colleague John had taken Peter directly to the nearest civilian hospital. After examining Peter, the doctors there had said that his arm would have to come off.

RAF North Weald – A Life Crisis

'No way,' Peter's colleague (who I now knew to be called John) had said. 'He is in the RAF and must be transferred to a service hospital.'

So, after the initial accident treatment, Peter had been transferred to RAF Halton and John had followed to make sure that he was in good hands. He'd then said that he would inform me of the accident.

In the event it would have been better for me to have had this information from the official channels. I learned later that John and Peter, after a hectic couple of days, had been very tired but wanted to get home. John had fallen asleep at the wheel and the car had hit a barrier. The passenger door on Peter's side had taken the full impact. John, who was not hurt, had recovered control of the car and, seeing that Peter was injured, had driven straight to the nearest hospital. He'd been glad when I appeared to accept the news calmly and had simply forgotten to give me particulars in his haste to get away.

Eventually we found the hospital that Peter was in but no details could be given over the phone except that he was in the operating theatre. This information made me worry even more.

I still had not shown any emotion and was going about doing things in a mechanical way. RAF transport was eventually arranged to take me to the hospital which was some distance away. On arrival they said they'd had to operate on Peter as his arm had a compound fracture and was hanging off. I found Peter in a semiconscious state as he had been given morphine. His arm was swathed in bandages. The only parts of his hand I could see were swollen and his fingers looked blue. The surgeon said it would be touch and go as to whether Peter would keep his arm but that he was trying his hardest to save it. I was relieved that Peter had no other injuries and his life was not threatened though

One Life

I was still desperately worried for him.

The cold winter days dragged on and the next weeks and months were some of the most difficult I had experienced, being both physically and mentally exhausting. Peter became very depressed at times. I'd drop everything and rush to the hospital to reassure him.

Getting to and from the hospital became a challenge as I had to make arrangements for Ruth and Christine to look after the children until I got home late in the evening. When I could not visit I tied a hot water bottle around my waist to keep me warm and went to the telephone box at a prearranged time. Then Peter would ring me from a mobile telephone box wheeled to his bedside having had to await his turn in the queue at his end. I'd queue, shivering outside the phone box in the dark. No mobile phones or nice warm quilted coats in those days!

Initially the surgeons were concerned with stitching Peter's arm back on and joining the severed nerve endings. This was pioneering surgery at that time. They also had to contend with the compound fractures and the lack of skin to cover the now oddly shaped elbow.

After recovering from one operation Peter tried to move his index finger but saw his middle finger move instead and panicked. The specialist said sorry but that they had joined the wrong tendons to the wrong fingers. They would operate again and sort it out. How lucky Peter was to be in the RAF as they would take all the time needed to save the arm.

The months passed and slowly the arm started to heal. It was during this time that Peter's pay was reduced on account of his hospital stay. With three small children to feed and clothe, I started dress making and taking in clothes requiring alterations. This was a skill I had learned from my mother.

RAF North Weald – A Life Crisis

I also answered an advert for sewing Binky baby pants. A gross of them (144) required elastic to be put in the waist and legs and I had to have them ready in a fortnight. I sewed from early morning to late evening. Jeanine, my two year old daughter, would crawl around the floor, sometimes sitting on my foot as it worked the pedal of the sewing machine. She would play for short periods happily but, like all very young children, she needed attention.

The plastic pants formed an ever mounting pile, creeping up the window in front of my machine. They then had to be trimmed and packed twelve at a time ready for collection. Ruth visited and brought Mandy with her to play with Jeanine. I worked late into the night whilst the children were in bed and Ruth often helped with the trimming around the legs. We had many laughs. Binky baby pants were not one of my most successful attempts at earning money. On checking and packing the first dozen we found some pants had acquired holes around the legs and waist from our trimming. 'So these are leaky baby pants,' we said, and we laughed. We agreed never, ever to buy a pair of Binky baby pants and decided the effort and time involved was not worth the pittance paid.

Next, I tried envelope addressing, still very poorly paid, but less arduous, and there was more time left to play with Jeanine. The days turned into weeks and the weeks into months. Despite having my two good friends I felt very lonely at times: their husbands were home most evenings and weekends.

As I've already said, Andrew was stubborn at times and had quite a temper. When cross with a toy he would stamp his feet, throw himself on the floor, or hit out at anyone close to him. I tended to give in to him. I was afraid that I may have inherited my mother's temper so did not like to get really cross with the children.

One Life

Then, at the school open day, I was shown some of Andrew's paintings. They had been displayed around the wall by his teacher and included paintings of horses and other animals. I thought them lifelike, artistically accurate, and in the correct scale in relation to their background.

Andrew's teacher said, 'It is very unusual for a boy of six years to produce paintings of this quality. He is an artistically gifted boy.' She added that, on the whole, she found him to be a polite and well behaved little boy, but that he could be 'quietly stubborn'. She said that sometimes he would look at her with his big blue eyes in an impudent way and that she'd found this difficult to handle. She wondered how I dealt with him. I agreed with her and said that I'd often felt exasperated by the looks he could give me. And, I told her about his temper tantrums.

'Would you like me to arrange an assessment by a child psychologist?' She asked. 'Gifted children usually do pose problems both at school and at home.'

I readily agreed.

In her assessment, the child psychologist agreed that Andrew was extremely artistic. I told her how I handled his tempers and she agreed that putting him on his own, away from everyone else, was the best way of dealing with him. 'You need to help him to control his temper or he will be extremely difficult to live with later. Artistic people can be quite selfish and demand a lot of attention.'

'Oh dear,' I thought, 'why can't I have a straight forward child?' I wished Peter was at home to give me support.

It was now Christmas and eight months since Peter's accident. There were presents and a tree to get. For the children this meant great excitement and Peter was allowed home for his first weekend. He now had a plaster cage around his chest to hold his

RAF North Weald – A Life Crisis

arm up and his clothes had been altered to accommodate this. The consultant decided that Peter, who was still worried about whether he had a future in the services, needed to come home for weekends in order to build up his confidence. His first trip home coincided with a heavy fall of snow and I was out with a shovel clearing the path in front of the house when he arrived. The children were very excited. They had only seen him on a few occasions due to the distance involved and, after the initial excitement and a cup of tea, he insisted on trying to finish clearing the path.

I protested, 'No you don't. You can't with one arm.'

The look he gave me spoke volumes about how he felt and so we all piled out to help. We must have looked a comical family, what with Peter, a shovel in his one good hand, trying hard not to overbalance, and the boys wrestling with a shovel almost as big as they were. I realised just how awful Peter must have been feeling about us having to manage without him.

The plaster cast was later removed and Peter was transferred to Headley Court, the famous RAF Rehabilitation Centre, where the aim was to restore service personnel, who had been injured, to full fitness. Peter would now be even further away, but would still be able to come home for occasional weekends.

Paul, a sensitive timid child, was even more subdued than usual and had tearful smudges around his eyes.

'What has happened?' I asked.

Andrew told me that a boy in Paul's class had thumped him on the back and called him names because he was small. 'I thumped him back,' Andrew said triumphantly, 'and told him not to touch my brother again.'

I had a chat with Paul and told him that if he just stood up for himself once with the name-caller he would be left alone. I

One Life

decided Paul had to be taught how to stand up for himself. This had come naturally to me as a child as it also seemed to have done for Andrew. I remembered when I had had to stand up to a bully when I was small, but Paul was such a gentle timid child that I was at a loss.

I asked my friends Bill and Stan to have a chat with Paul and they did talk with him and showed him how to stand up for himself.

I thought about how I had dodged my mother's clouts and how I had come to expect being clouted. In fact, I had got so used to it that I just came to accept it as part of my daily routine. Verbal intimidation affected me far more. I'd developed strategies for dealing with her rising temper and her bullying and violence towards me. Dealing with my peers was altogether different: I had no fear in facing and dealing with them.

When, a few days later, another scuffle with the boys at school took place, Paul came home triumphant. He had stood his ground with the bully. I can't remember an occasion when Paul ever had to resort to fighting back after that.

About this time I started to suffer from severe headaches and was losing a lot of weight. I hadn't seen Peter's parents since our short stay in the transit camp at Blackpool on arrival back from Malta. I don't think I ever thought about having a mother around for encouragement, advice and support at this time. They knew about Peter's accident but I didn't tell them about the difficulties I was having. I didn't want to worry them and I also didn't want them to think I couldn't cope. Ruth asked me whether my mother would be coming to see me and help out. I brushed the question aside saying she did not keep in contact. Ruth and Christine were there but I never asked for their help unless it was for the children. I wanted to try and cope by myself. I felt that I must

RAF North Weald – A Life Crisis

cope, or be a failure as a mother.

Then, just as Peter began to recover from his injury, there began a period when the pain and sickness from headaches, and consequent blackouts, crept gradually and stealthily into my daily life. The past months had been spent in looking after the children, doing all sorts of extra jobs to earn the money we needed to get by on, and visiting Peter to try and keep his spirits up.

There was a throbbing, sickening pain in my head on getting up in the morning and this was accompanied by zigzag lines in front of my eyes which had become very sensitive to light. I would vomit and retch until I felt so bad I could have cheerfully put my head down the toilet and flushed the chain. The persistence and severity of these attacks varied, but I had to get up and carry on with getting Jeanine up, fed, and into her play pen and the boys off to school.

I tried various remedies although these just made me feel sicker. I told no one about the headaches for fear that they would think me neurotic. I just wanted to crawl into bed and lie there, but I couldn't, not with three children and a house to run. The attacks could last for two to three days. Sometimes vomiting would relieve the pain for a short while, but I could not eat when having these attacks. Gradually I lost more and more weight and started having dizzy spells. I started to become depressed about life in general.

The periods in between attacks were wonderful. Waking up free of a headache I would try and catch up with everything and make it up to the children. I felt really guilty about them. Soon though the bad days became more regular and, with my general health deteriorating, and my drastic loss of weight, it became a nightmare world for me.

I retreated more and more into myself and my self esteem was

One Life

very low. I felt unworthy of my good friends, and therefore I tried to avoid them. The dizzy attacks became more frequent. Sometimes I even fell over. One day Ruth and Christine called to see me and, finding the door open, they were shocked at finding me unconscious at the foot of the stairs with a convector heater beside me. Jeanine was sitting by me, stroking my face. There was blood on my lip and I had an ugly lump on this side my head.

After a while I started to come round, though I was still disorientated and groggy. Christine went round to the phone box to call the doctor and Ruth waited with me until he arrived. I was upset being such a nuisance. Ruth told me how worried both she and Christine had been.

'Look at you,' she said. 'You're just skin and bone. What is wrong with you?'

I told her about the awful headaches and the dizzy spells.

'You should have told us before and we would have seen you went to the doctor's,' she said. When the doctor arrived he examined me and said I was probably just anaemic and exhausted I was to go to bed and stay there for at least 48 hours. He gave me a capsule to take immediately and a prescription for more.

I was not to know then what a disastrous effect these sodium amatol tablets would have on me. Christine had her doubts, even at this early-stage, though the immediate problem was to get me to bed before the capsule the doctor had given me had time to take effect. Relaxed, and becoming sleepy, I made no protest.

Ruth and Christine organised the children's care between them and decided that leaving the door unlocked was the safest option, I would sleep heavily on the medication and they'd look in on me later. They could manage this for 48 hours and it would give them time to get in touch with my relatives.

RAF North Weald – A Life Crisis

Ruth later found my mother's telephone number in my address book. She took Paul with her to the phone box since she felt that my mother might want to speak to him and reassure him. My mother answered and Ruth introduced herself and said that I was ill and needed help. To Ruth's amazement my mother replied that she couldn't care less if I died so long as she did not have to bury me. Then she told Ruth not to ring again and slammed the phone down. Ruth was aghast and related the conversation to Christine. Both of them couldn't believe that a mother could be so wickedly uncaring.

Peter's parents were not on the telephone so Christine and Ruth decided to see how things were after I'd rested for a while before contacting Peter, who was still undergoing treatment at Headley Court. There was a chance he might even be home for a weekend. Ruth called back later that evening and, on being roused, I ranted and raved, believing in my drugged state that she was my mother. I even threw an alarm clock at her. Ruth retreated hastily. Later I was told that I'd had had a 'regression back into my childhood.' They believed me to be revolting against my mother's treatment in a way in which I had never been able to do in reality.

After a good rest I did feel a little better but the medication was knocking me out. I found it difficult to get up in the mornings and the headaches got even worse. I did not realise it was the medication that was making the headaches worse. I suffered more blackouts and consequently more bruises that I could not account for. Christine had her suspicions about these blackouts and insisted I tell the doctor. He examined me and made an appointment for me to go into hospital for a day and have an electroencephalograph taken.

Peter's Mum and Dad came up for a couple of days and I went

One Life

in for the tests. The specialist told me I was suffering from chronic migraines and that these could bring on a type of epileptic fit. He gave me medication for the migraines, and the fits, and arranged for me to come back in a fortnight for further tests.

I was shocked and devastated. I just could not take it in. I sat in numbed silence on the way home. Peter's mum was shocked too.

'It can't be right,' she said. 'You just get on with life, and eat properly, and you will get better. Never mind what the doctors says. Peter needs a wife that can cope and can care, both for him and for his children.'

She then went into town, taking Jeanine with her.

That night despairing thoughts just went round and around in my mind. All I could think of was that I was an epileptic who had fits. I was useless: no good to anybody.

The next day I continued to feel miserable and useless. I made a cup of tea and sat down opposite Peter's dad who was now blind and hoping to get a guide dog soon.

We drank our tea in silence and then Dad said, 'Mum's right: you are no use to yourself, Peter, or the children. He deserves better. He needs a wife that puts him first. He would be better off without you.'

On hearing this I ran upstairs. I thought, he's right, Peter would be better off without me, and so would the children, and he'd soon find a new wife – a wife that does deserve him!

In my befuddled mind this all seemed logical. I'd get myself out of the way. I'd take all those capsules. I found them in the cabinet in the bathroom and carefully took some. I'd take the rest with another cup of tea. I went down stairs to where Dad was. Sitting down I gradually emptied the bottle with my tea.

RAF North Weald – A Life Crisis

Dad was still mumbling on at me and I retorted quietly, 'Don't you worry yourself. I'll be out of the way soon enough.'

Dad must gradually have realised that something was wrong. Probably I sounded strange. He shouted at me, 'What's wrong with you?'

Then, becoming a little concerned when I didn't answer, he made his way over to Ruth's and she came back with him,

'I didn't mean it,' he said despairingly, as Ruth took one look at me and then the empty pill bottle. She shot off to ring for an ambulance. I was rushed off into hospital and had my stomach pumped. I didn't come round properly for a couple of days.

'Hello, Sleeping Beauty,' the woman in the next bed said.

I turned away feeling very sorry for myself. I couldn't even get this right.

'Oh, come on, Love,' the woman said. 'Your husband has been at your bedside night and day. He has only just gone off to get changed. He won't be long. I thought you were only a fifteen year old girl when they brought you in, you looked so small and pale.'

It had been touch and go for a while and they still weren't sure if any damage had been caused to my system.

Then Peter arrived, 'Don't you ever do anything like that to me again,' he said, as I burst into tears. 'I couldn't live without you and neither could the children. We all love you very much. Dad told us what he said to you. He didn't mean it. He and Mum were just so shocked. They love you really.'

I sobbed, 'But I'm no use to any of you.'

'Listen,' he said, 'I love you. It doesn't matter to me what's wrong with you. You've been there for me these past months and it didn't matter to you whether I'd end up one-armed. Just my being alive was what mattered to you after my accident and I

One Life

could not have got better if you hadn't been there for me. I'm not surprised you got rundown with all you had to cope with.'

We talked at length and I began to see what a mistake I had made. He said I was not to worry, that the boys were OK with Joan and David, and that Mum and Dad were with Jeanine at home. I was to get myself well and not worry about anything for a while.

A specialist came to see me later and said and I was lucky to be in a hospital that specialised in neurological problems. I'd have to stay in for some weeks and would need further tests to find out just what caused these fits. He explained I had suffered very mild 'petit mal fits' which was a type of hysterical fit. He said that during a migraine my brain became hysterical and could not cope with the overload. He added, 'Think of it as an electric current going through a wire. Then a break in the wire occurs and everything breaks down and goes haywire. These episodes can be controlled with medication. Also, before being discharged, you must put on a stone in weight. Do you know that you only weigh five stone? After the tests have finished I shall be putting you on Insulin to help you gain weight fast. But first I want to see how you are with no treatment, monitor a migraine and fit, and get another encephalograph reading.'

He explained everything so well that I felt a lot better.

I stayed in the hospital for eight weeks. Before the insulin treatment could start I had a series of tests. Pat, the cheerful light hearted woman in the next bed to mine, had a genetic neurological disorder. All around me were people with such awful neurological conditions, some awaiting test results for dreadful uncontrollable fits. I felt ashamed that I had felt so miserable about my condition and was soon up and about and helping with little things for those unable to get out of bed.

RAF North Weald – A Life Crisis

During one of my sick headaches the doctor attached electrodes to monitor my brain activity. Then I had a migraine, followed by a fit, and there were more tests, including a lumbar puncture. This was an experience I would not wish on anyone.

Finally the specialist told me that the migraines and fits were a delayed result of the meningitis I had suffered as a child and that my drastic loss of weight had triggered them. The good news was that this could all be put right by putting me on insulin treatment.

This was, for me, the turning point. A concerted effort would now be made to get me fit and well and back to my family. I started to eat properly. I even put things in my dressing gown pockets to try and further increase my readings when I was weighed, but they soon rumbled me, and after that I was frisked regularly! I felt I could give something back, and now tried to comfort and help the other patients. This, in turn, did a great deal to help me.

Peter had now been discharged from Headley Court with enough movement of his arm to enable him to stay in the in the RAF. I left hospital with instructions to keep up the high protein diet. I was so glad to be back at home with Peter, whose parents had returned home the day before, his mum feeling that I would need peace and quiet to settle down. But Ruth and Christine soon came over and were pleased at how much better I looked. And then the boys returned too.

I talked with Peter openly. He had his own anxieties and needed to get his confidence back. At last I had learned that I was not alone in my sufferings and that what I had thought my own particular demons were in fact no way unique. We all have our good and our bad times. Maybe some other folk are better at putting up a front though now I'm far from sure that that is a good idea. And soon after this we started to arrange a dinner to

One Life

thank our friends.

However, before arrangements could be made Peter was again posted this time to High Wycombe Bentley Priory. My friends said not to worry, we can come to your new home and combine it with a house warming.

Chapter Sixteen

High Wycombe Bentley Priory

We soon settled into the lovely surroundings here, with two friendly neighbours next door, and held a combined house warming and the thank you dinner celebration we'd planned.

Friends at our celebration thank you, and Peter relaxing with Stan.

Then, soon after this, Peter was posted to India for six months to help with organising a sanitation plant. My doctor was all for stopping this posting, so soon after my recovery, stating that I was not, as yet, fully well. But I insisted that Peter be allowed to go; he needed this prestigious job to gain back his self confidence.

My doctor was still unhappy but could do nothing without my co-operation. I have never regretted making this choice. Although it was to be difficult for me I felt that otherwise Peter would always regret missing the chance to prove himself. I remembered Peter's parents' bitterness at giving up their respective ambitions.

Once again, the evenings were the times when I missed Peter

One Life

the most, especially those following the short, cold, dull, grey days of winter. I wasn't sleeping too well over this period and would often get up during the night and fill the time doing something.

I tried my hand at woodwork and made Jeanine a cupboard for her socks and ribbons out of a wine box. I covered the box in stick-fast plastic, making a little curtain for the front. However my attempt at shortening a high stool by cutting off part of the legs was not a success. It wobbled hideously and so I gave up woodwork. Thankfully, summer was soon upon us, bringing plenty to do again.

It was about this time that I was asked if I would be a NAAFI representative for the RAF personnel on camp. I had to check that the items displayed in the shop were useful to the airman and note any complaints and suggestions. Not only did I enjoy this task but I also learned a great deal about comparing prices and goods.

After Peter had left for India I had more problems with Andrew. Paul was now at junior school whilst Andrew was at a different primary school. They were collected and taken by their schools by bus. Andrew started saying he didn't want to go to school, because he didn't feel well, and he certainly seemed to be running a temperature. This went on for a couple of days but I couldn't find anything specifically wrong with him.

So the next time Andrew ran a temperature I called the doctor who, after carrying out a thorough examination, said there was nothing wrong with him and that he was just working up a temperature so as not to go to school. It appeared that he did not like going to a different school to Paul. The doctor told him he had to go to school the next day and not cause his mummy any more problems.

High Wycombe Bentley Priory

The very next day, after I saw him off on the bus which dropped him at his school. He then waited for the bus to leave and promptly walked back home! I phoned the school and took him in myself.

I found out later that Paul was getting off the bus with Andrew, seeing him into the primary school, and then walking on to his own school not much further down the road. Despite this he was never late and I thought he was showing a responsibility for his brother well beyond his years.

It was not long after this that I received a note requesting that I call in at Paul's school regarding his progress. The head teacher said that, on being tested, Paul had shown above average intelligence for a seven year old and yet his reading ability was below average. I explained that, conscious of my own educational shortcomings, I had left all these matters to the school. At a previous school I'd been told that parents could confuse children if they attempted to teach them using the wrong methods. The head said that on Paul's return to school after the summer break they would carry out more tests and see what they could do. He was obviously such a bright child that it seemed a real shame.

This started me on a new course of action. I went to the local library and shops, looking for anything to do with children learning to read, and found a bookshop specialising in specific teaching aids as used in schools. There were flash cards, Early Reader books, Ladybird books, and others. The Ladybird books at one shilling and sixpence, with both pictures and words, looked ideal, whilst the Early Reader books had less obvious words to match the pictures. The Flash Cards, with single large printed words on each card, helped in word recognition, I looked around at home to see what else I could use.

One Life

Throughout the long summer holidays I earmarked two hours a day for learning. If the previous school had failed to teach the boys then I was going to have a jolly good try. And I would find a way of helping them catch up.

We had great fun. We played spelling games, like 'I spy with my little eye... a "C A R P E T",' holding up the flash cards so that the boys could identify the one with the correct word printed upon it. We carried on with this method until just about all our available household items could be identified by the words on the flash cards.

There were little prizes and treats for success, and encouragement when they made mistakes. I realised that young children could only really sustain full attention in ten minute bursts so I broke up the time with other more fun things to do. I promised both of the boys a watch if they learned to tell the time before the new term. The flash cards were invaluable and they soon used the pictures to start reading from the Ladybird books.

We used an egg timer to teach the time. I taught them how to draw a circle and divide it into four, recognising that each sector represented a quarter of an hour or fifteen minutes, and we did jobs together and timed just how long each job took. We also set time tables for learning time and playing time, and went on outings – remembering to spell-out the words for animals or things we'd seen.

Paul's first real success came when out on a bus one day. On passing a building he asked me, 'What does "P R U D E N T I A L" mean, Mummy?' He was off, and he never looked back: he read anything and everything.

Andrew was less keen on reading. Although he did learn and perform well, he was not really bothered about it, and only read when asked to do so, but they both learned to tell the time, and

High Wycombe Bentley Priory

were presented with their watches, which was an extra bonus.

Not to be left out Jeanine also learned to read and I realised that you don't need to be a teacher, or highly educated, to teach young children. All one really needed was some common savvy, enthusiasm, organisational skill, and to mix in some fun.

When Paul went back after the holidays I was again summoned to the school. Wondering what on earth could be wrong now I found only a very puzzled head teacher. She said that, far from needing special extra tuition, Paul now showed an ability to read well within his age group. I explained that I had taught him.

'But how?' she asked, patronisingly. 'You yourself told me you had no education.'

I had, I said, used teaching aids available to anyone.

'But you're not a teacher,' she expostulated.

I replied I now believed that, as a parent, I had an advantage in being able to teach my own child on a one to one basis.

Never again would I allow my children's education to suffer because of my lack of input, even if I did have to learn a subject first. I'd discovered that a parent can also be invaluable as a teacher. I'd identified a problem and not been afraid to do something about it. Patronising attitudes from others towards us parents is not helpful.

I still suffered migraines and had the occasional fit but I kept these well hidden until one day, on coming in from school and pushing at the front door, Paul found it wouldn't open. Giving it a good push, with Andrew's assistance, he found me on the floor with the fingers of one hand trapped under the door. He tried to wake me, pulling my hand free and pushing me onto my side, before running next door for Gladys. Fortunately she was home from her part time job.

One Life

I was beginning to come round as she arrived and she gave me such a rollicking for not telling her that I had these fits. Paul himself did not know much about them. She said I owed a responsibility to my children and friends and needed to be more trusting.

I apologised. We talked together and I told her how I felt. I confessed my fear that, if people knew about the fits, I would be labelled and held back in what I did. She said that, whilst she did understand this, I needed to trust those close to me to keep the secret. She asked me why I always wore dark glasses, even on a cloudy day. I explained that this was to reduce the frequency of my migraines. I said that I had got used to the strange looks I got from other people and was so very much better these days, with fewer attacks.

Later, I said I would like to do something to enable me to take a part time job and she suggested I go on a course with her to brush up my typing skills. The course was held at a college in Watford in the evenings and Gladys was due to start her second term the following week. Feeling that if I could get away with dark glasses on an evening course at the college with fluorescent lighting, I could cope with anything, I joined Gladys on the course and this proved to be very useful.

I had regular letters from Peter and keeping busy helped the time pass. I also took a real interest in my mature garden at the front of the house. I knew nothing about gardening, but I soon found myself becoming involved. I had a variety of flowers and shrubs, and even a row of strawberries.

Both Gladys and her husband Jim were keen gardeners. He worked on night shifts, coming home to bed at six in the morning, before getting up again midmorning to potter about in his garden. He would lean over the fence and tell me what to

High Wycombe Bentley Priory

prune and how to look after the strawberries. Then we started having coffee together when he got up before working in our gardens. Squirrels and rabbits visited so we had to protect the strawberries. The milkman would call and say, 'Won't be long now. You will need some cream to go with those strawberries.'

Gladys worked part time in the village and was usually home by 4 p.m. She had two teenage daughters who were at an argumentative age. Jim grumbled good-naturedly that he was constantly surrounded by women in his house. I was lucky, he said, to have two boys who never appeared to fight.

'Paul will not fight with anyone,' I said. 'He likes a quiet life and keeps out of Andrew's way if he is in a mood.'

Then Jeanine started ballet school. I wanted her to be able to grasp all the opportunities open to her, and ballet taught her balance and confidence. The boys had to accompany me and wait for her class to finish. Noticing Andrew tapping his feet to the music, the teacher asked him if he would like to join in. Being the only boy did not deter him and he joined in happily. He was a natural and appeared to enjoy himself. Soon Paul also joined in and, although he had less talent than Andrew, he appeared to enjoy himself too.

I bought tap and ballet shoes for all three. I was already making dresses for Jeanine and myself and now I made her little ballet dresses. A show was due to be put on at Watford College by the dancing school in aid of Children's Charities, and on July 4th 1964, all three of mine took part. Andrew and Paul were Humpty Dumpty's children. Being the only boys, they were made a great fuss of. The experience would, I thought, give the children confidence in performing before an audience.

On my birthday in August I received a single rose in a long box from Peter. It was a lovely surprise. I was putting on

One Life

weight, becoming much fitter, and gaining confidence in bringing up the children and coping with their problems. Even before he'd gone to India, Peter and I had agreed that, what with him being away all week, I would not 'save up' any naughty behaviour and ask him to deal with it at the weekends. I made sure that the boy's always understood just why they were being punished.

Time passed and Peter came home, having thoroughly enjoyed his time in India. He was now full of confidence in his ability to do his job and had gained a commendation from the Air Officer Commanding in recognition of the excellent work he had done. We were all very proud of him. It was lovely to have Peter home with me and to see him so tanned, healthy, happy and confident. Paul had his eighth birthday just after Peter got back.

Life was good.

On Peter's return from leave he was told he was posted to RAF Muharraq in Bahrain and that I would be able to join him there. This was a real privilege as only selected strategic personnel could have their wives with them. He was to depart the following month, and just as soon as a flat could be found for us, and passports, visas, inoculations and the like sorted out, I would follow with the children.

Soon packing started in earnest. I had to have a health check and clearance for me to travel. With my new born confidence, and the performance of our 'marching out' from our quarter accomplished, we all set off to Brize Norton for the exiting flight to Bahrain.

What new adventures lay ahead? I wondered.

Chapter Seventeen

Bahrain 1965

We arrived at Bahrain Airport after a very long tiring flight and the heat enveloped us as we descended the aircraft steps. So this is Bahrain, I thought. I had so looked forward to coming. Bahrain, meaning 'The Two Seas' owing to its geographical position in the Arabian Gulf, was the natural stopping place for air services between the Middle and Far East. Ruled then by Sheikh Isa Bin Sulman Al Khalifah, this independent Arab state consisted of an archipelago of small low-lying islands half way along the Arabian Gulf.

Peter was waiting for us at the airport and there were hugs and kisses all round. We were anxious to see him after the three months we had been apart. To be coming to such an exciting place was an added bonus. The ride in the taxi was not too long and soon we arrived at our new flat at Almahooz, Manamah. The

Flats on the old race course

flat, very spacious, well furnished, and air conditioned, was part of a block that had been newly built on what had been the old

One Life

The women's mosque (centre).

race course. There were villages nearby and we were able to watch local life going on at a distance.

We could also see the women's mosque, as in the photograph. Women were not allowed to go to the men's mosque. I was to find out more about the customs later.

Andrew looking at the dates laid out on the ground to dry.

Bahrain 1965

Peter had a number of local men in his Health and Sanitation Team and was responsible for a large area. This included a number of date groves where their job was to combat the risk of malaria by using fog sprays to kill the mosquitoes.

Mamood offers Peter a drink of coffee.

These date groves produced a great number of dates. The local men would shin up the tree, bring down the clumps of dates, and then lay them out on the ground to dry. There were also little stalls where they would offer us coffee. When offered a second coffee we always had to accept it so as not to cause them offence. After that we were allowed to just shake the cup from side to side to politely say no thank you. The drinking of coffee was a tradition in Bahrain. Peter's role included liaising with the locals including the Sheikh himself who was very happy in the way Peter carried out his job. The Sheikh showed his appreciation by sending fresh vegetables to our flat on a regular basis.

Peter showed us how hot Bahrain was by cracking an egg on a stone slab. It fried in a couple of minutes, much to the amusement of the children. The children started attending the RAF school at Muharraq, just across the causeway from Manamah.

I acquired a domestic servant who had been recommended to Peter by a colleague. He came from Zanzibar, where they still chopped off your hands if you were caught stealing, and had previously worked in the Airmen's Mess. Consequently he had learned most of his English from our lads, but I soon re-educated him! He was very good; he had an excellent way of being invisible when working around the house and was never intrusive. I had been a little nervous about having a male servant; however in Bahrain the women were not allowed to work and so men covered all areas of employment. He did all the housework, washing and ironing, and also taught me useful words to use in the local souk market where bartering was the norm. He said I should always take one of the boys with me, if Peter was not able to accompany me, as having a boy with you gave you respectability. I would not then be annoyed by unwanted attention. This information was useful and helped me to acquire some good bargains whilst in Bahrain.

Deep into the old souk.

I enjoyed shopping in the souk with its profusion of colours, sounds, and aromatic aromas. Occasionally, and in certain parts of the souk, you might see the odd rat scurrying past, and it was here that usually only the locals ventured. Nevertheless, and despite the bartering becoming very much more serious, it was here that I purchased items much more cheaply.

We saw Arab smiths making tins by hand in the iron foundry and watched the skilful fashioning of brasses, marvelled at the wood carving, and experienced the culture.

I bought a sewing machine and did dressmaking for the other wives. This earned me the money to buy other things that I could

Bahrain 1965

Family outing to sea.

never have got in England. Many wives did not like the idea of male shop keepers measuring them for clothes.

We had days out at sea. We all enjoyed swimming, and the boys were good at it, though they still wore rubber rings as a safety precaution. One day a friendly porpoise appeared by Paul and playfully rubbed up against him. Both boy and fish were happy with this until suddenly the porpoise's rough skin burst Paul's ring. I do not know which of them was the more startled! Paul pulled himself out of the sea and the porpoise just circled the boat for a while before finally swimming away.

I had started to use colour slide films in my camera, so that when I went home I could show relatives slide shows. We accumulated many slides showing a broad flavour of Bahrain.

The Bahrain people were very welcoming, friendly and honest. They opened up their homes to us and invited us to their weddings and celebrations. Their customs were very different from ours and we made sure that we learned about them before visiting. They never gave specific times to visit when giving us an invitation, but were insulted if it didn't take place soon. We had to use the left hand when eating and when taking our shoes off to wash our feet before entering a house. The women always sat in a different room from the men, although, as their honoured guest, I would be expected to sit with the men. I paid special attention to my dress and made sure my arms and legs were covered. These were, to me, common courtesies and not a problem. In return I was able to share their confidences, and learn about their life, and this gave me a better understanding of the Arab culture.

My health had improved immensely. I still had the occasional migraine but the medication appeared to be keeping the fits under control. I had an ergametrin medihaler and took migralive tablets when a migraine did occur. My secret never spread beyond the family and a very few real friends. I was sure that if people knew my secret their attitude towards me would change.

Soon after arriving in Bahrain, the duty MO, insisted on changing my medication and this had disastrous consequences for me. Once again I ended up in hospital for 48 hours being given injections. The consultant in the hospital told me that he too suffered with migraines and understood what I went through.

'I can't tell you how glad I am to hear this,' I said. 'If you, as a consultant, also suffer with them then I cannot be just a stupid neurotic person.'

He laughed at this, saying that people who suffered with migraines were often very intelligent people and were certainly not stupid. He asked about my attacks and if I had many fits these days. I replied that I had only occasional migraines and

Bahrain 1965

grudgingly admitted to a couple of fits. He said then that my medication should not have been changed and that he would speak to the MO. He then saw from my notes that I was allergic to eggs. This had been discovered earlier when I first arrived in Bahrain and, having suffered toothache, had some teeth out. I had reacted to the injection which apparently contained egg. He reminded me not to eat eggs under any circumstances.

This stay in hospital brought about a full apology from the doctor who'd changed the medication, but I still didn't like admitting to anyone that I suffered from migraines. Later I came across a doctor and a dentist who both had migraine attacks and they introduced me to the Migraine Trust. I was given copies of the Trust magazines which were edited by a man in Bournemouth. The magazines were interesting and carried news of research. They were also uplifting; each of their writers obviously had a very good sense of humour. Th magazine printed reports and tips from readers. It helped me to keep things in perspective and I learned how to deal with this intruder into my life. And it helped me get through the bad days. At least the migraines would pass and were not life threatening. I made up for losing a day or two by enjoying the wonderful days in between the attacks with their freedom from pain. How lucky I was to have help in the house! The doctor and dentist told me they did lose working days, but that was just life. On one of my visits the doctor asked me to take my glasses off and used a tuning fork behind both my ears. He told me that he was sure that my hearing was not as good as it should be.

'My hearing is better than most,' I retorted.

'You won't mind going for a test then will you? We will have to fly you to Aden for this. Peter can accompany you.'

Peter said it explained a good deal. We flew over the Empty

One Life

Quarter and took some good camera shots. It is a desolate place and it was no surprise to be told that if we crashed there would be no way that we could survive.

Worryingly, on landing in Aden, I stood up, felt dizzy, and an ambulance was called. In hospital tests were carried out on my ears and the consultant said that I had certain hearing losses at both high and low levels. He added that the dizziness had been brought on by the balance in my inner ears being affected and was nothing to worry about.

'Why can I hear things across the room when others cannot?' I asked. He replied that it seemed likely that I was probably quite adept at lip reading and that sometimes people who were losing their hearing developed this skill naturally. It was also probable that I concentrated more on people's faces when in conversation with them, and listened more carefully, especially where there was background noise. In particular the noise from air conditioning would certainly make things much more difficult for me. Then he told me not to worry but just to be aware of the problem and to ensure others were aware too. Later I might need a hearing aid and must keep my glasses up to date so that I could see well.

My suffering had been much worse with my migraines and fits and so I felt, as we left to go to our hotel for the night, that I could discount this. As we walked along the road I noticed sandbags around the doors and soldiers with guns. Then, from not far behind us, there came a load explosion! We hid behind the sandbags surrounding the doorway of a building.

'What was that?' I said.

'I don't know,' Peter replied, 'but we are staying put until we find out.'

I knew they'd had some trouble here in Aden but that

Bahrain 1965

explosion had been too close for comfort. Solders were rushing about everywhere. We moved inside an hotel until things quietened down. Later we heard that a Land-Rover had been blown up. This trip was turning out to be an eventful one.

We flew back next day to Bahrain. I relaxed and was taking things easy. The medication I had been given had made me a little unsteady on my feet but I managed to get home under my own steam. I often found flying affected me slightly, but fortunately this was not usually noticeable to others. Peter joked that I must have had too much tipple.

The Sheikh extended an invitation to certain families of service men to use the long stretch of the seashore in front of his beach house. Arab women were not allowed to swim and this included female children. We were introduced to the Sheikh himself, who sometimes frequented the beach, and this was a special privilege. He would sometimes join us at our table. After

Peter with Jeanine at the Sheikh's beach.

201

One Life

one such meeting Jeanine and I were invited to have a look around his palace. We were escorted by his man-servant Mohammed who would often bring afternoon tea out to us on the beach. The water was crystal clear, and very warm, and the beach was of soft white sand. We all had a marvellous time.

I needed to become independent within my marriage if I was to have any sort of enjoyable life. With Peter away so much, I needed my own hobbies and needed to make my own friends. I'm an outgoing go-getter sort of a person. Although it's by no means simple to start new ventures, ideas often come easily to me. Even so, I often had to psych myself up to tackle novel situations. I found I could do this by throwing myself in at the deep end. I'd enjoy going to after-show parties quite happily, with or without Peter when he was away.

Peter was very good on social occasions. People found him likeable, easy to get on with, and a kind and caring person. He also enjoyed acting and performing and was a good stage manager. He could talk anyone into anything and his staff liked and respected him. In addition he had the gift of the gab and could stand up and give a talk on almost any subject with little or no preparation.

I had good support from Peter when he was there. We joined The 'Alpha Players', a theatre group which was one of the many to be found on most RAF stations. Their membership was diverse and ranged across all ranks and cultures. Consequently one would hear many different accents, not only those we are all so familiar with from the many and diverse dialects found in England, but also from our many colonies and dominions abroad. This made the whole experience even more fascinating, interesting and enjoyable. The MO both acted in and produced our plays. These clubs always flourished and provided a great

Bahrain 1965

source of diverse entertainment and satisfaction for us all.

The facilities for our dramatic endeavours differed from camp to camp. Sometimes there was a full-blown theatre and stage lighting and at others existing NAAFI premises would be used if they had a stage. Our plays were put on to a paying audience and were expected to be of a high standard. Our group had a mixed membership which – due to our postings here, there and everywhere of service personnel – was constantly changing. As well as learning how to be convincing actors we all had to learn the many skills required for the vital backstage work of wardrobe, props, and stage management. There was always a need for new blood; anyone interested was always welcome and would learn alongside the rest of us.

Unlike Peter, I preferred to keep a low profile on joining a new club. I had found that sitting back gave me an opportunity to observe just how things were. We had play readings which I enjoyed. Often, we would be laughing out loud so much as we acted out our parts, regardless of whether the play was supposed to be serious or a comedy, that we could hardly read.

A good producer could be in place for several plays so, regarding this role, opportunities for newcomers arose rarely. However small test plays were produced and directed by newcomers. These were shown only to club members for adjudication. A producer had to have a good track record as we played to paying audiences and large amounts of money were involved. Our plays had to be produced to a professional standard.

I helped with make-up, wardrobe, prompting, in front of house with Peter, and of course acting, although acting was not my preferred choice. I was more interested in the production and directing side of things. I studied all aspects of dramatic

One Life

presentation, learned many new techniques and very much enjoyed the camaraderie and team spirit. With so many colourful characters amongst our actors the after-show parties were often as good as the show itself. And, for me, the best was still to come.

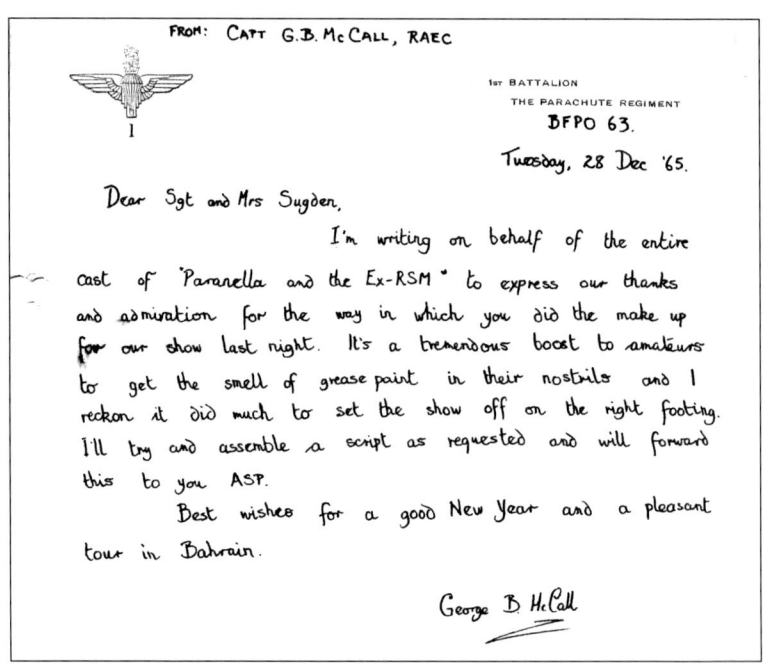

> FROM: CAPT G.B. McCALL, RAEC
>
> 1st BATTALION
> THE PARACHUTE REGIMENT
> BFPO 63.
>
> Tuesday, 28 Dec '65.
>
> Dear Sgt and Mrs Sugden,
>
> I'm writing on behalf of the entire cast of 'Paranella' and the Ex-RSM" to express our thanks and admiration for the way in which you did the make up for our show last night. It's a tremendous boost to amateurs to get the smell of grease paint in their nostrils and I reckon it did much to set the show off on the right footing. I'll try and assemble a script as requested and will forward this to you ASP.
>
> Best wishes for a good New Year and a pleasant tour in Bahrain.
>
> George B McCall

Army letter

Peter and I were contacted by the Army requesting us to do the make-up for their entertainment lads who were due to be ashore in the desert over Christmas. They were putting on a pantomime, with an all-male cast, and make-up was needed. They collected us and brought us back. The experience was interesting and enjoyable.

I took up tennis and joined the choral society, and continued with theatre activities. I had done the make-up for one of their

Bahrain 1965

shows. Now I was back in a choir. The last time I had been in a choir was at church some years previously. The choir performed in many and varied places singing excerpts from operettas and musicals including *Tell me little Maiden*. Mike Walker, conductor of the Manamah Society, was well-known as a musician and choirmaster with his wife as his pianist.

The children were growing fast. They boys were now in the Wolf Cubs and the Swimming Club. Initially, I didn't know what to do about Jeanine. There was no dancing school in Bahrain and she missed it. Then the Sheikh said he would like his daughter to take up ballet and so the CO's wife, who had been a dancing teacher, decided to start up a ballet school. I helped out with the baby class, which Jeanine attended, and even ran the class myself on a couple of occasions.

These were my first independent hobbies, without even Peter's involvement. As a service wife, I was later to realise the positive effect this could have on a husband's career! We also felt some responsibility towards those RAF personnel who were not allowed to bring their wives with them.

At Christmas and New Year we opened our flat to entertain some of these lonely lads. Peter had bought a tape recorder and speakers, and he would DJ the dancing. This was his big hobby then. We'd lay on food and fun was had by all. This included the children, who, on waking up, would jump over the back of the sofas and on to the bodies sleeping off the revelries of the night before. No one seemed to mind this and at least it must have given them a feeling of at least being with a family for a short while.

Some of the party food for the buffet came from the Sheikh who'd sent salad and fruit to our flat every week. At Christmas he'd send us a Christmas tree, fruit, and dates as well. We were

One Life

very lucky. Fresh produce had to be flown in from a country with a cooler climate, and was therefore very expensive.

Toys that were far too expensive in England were easily affordable there in Bahrain. Jeanine had a talking doll and the boys got fire engines and aeroplanes. Buying presents to send to relatives was a joy. Monthly supplies of drink, which were rationed and for servicemen only, were collected from the mess stores. Selling or giving alcohol to the local people was a very serious offence and we were warned that any offenders would be charged and posted home forthwith in disgrace. They could also expect to face the full rigour of the Bahrain justice system. This was a dry country where drink was against their Muslim religion.

Drinking in the mess was a social occasion. As we started work early, and usually finished by 2 p.m., visiting the mess for a drink during the day became the norm, and Peter was not an exception.

This gradually became a problem over the years and put a strain on our marriage. It was brought home to me when a friend of mine, who also taught Andrew at school, suggested I look at his drawing book on the next open day. On the subject of 'my dad and what he does off duty', Andrew had drawn a picture of Peter snoring in an arm chair with a cigarette hanging from the fingers of one hand and a beer glass clasped in the other. Although funny at the time it was but a foretaste of what might well be to come.

Peter was often away visiting Dubai and other places and, as an RAF wife, I was expected to cope with the family alone. When some shooting trouble broke out around the causeway connecting Muharraq with Manamah, we families were all told to stay in our homes. Food and other necessities were brought in for the army wives, but no one thought to check on the RAF wives. I

Bahrain 1965

decided to venture out across the racecourse to go to the shops and, looking back, was probably very lucky to return safely.

Then there was the time when a neighbour knocked on my door saying a man had got into her flat to steal. Armed only with a tennis racket, out I rushed, into her flat and up onto the roof where he had been seen last. What I would have done if I had met up with him I've no idea. Fortunately, the robber had gone. I was obviously very foolish in those days.

There were far more male personnel around than females. Two lads who became firm friends and glad of a little home comfort were often at our flat. Sometimes they would baby sit for us. Women did not go around unaccompanied in Bahrain: it was just not done. So I provided company and friendship for John, a shy, thoughtful young man, who was good with the children.

John spent a lot of time with us and accompanied the children and me to the beach on several occasions whilst Peter was away. I didn't notice that he was developing a crush on me and he certainly never behaved in such a manner as to cause me to be uncomfortable. Then, one evening, we arrived back at the flat from the beach and, after settling the children in bed, we sat, as we often did, listening to classical music before it was time for him to return to camp. Suddenly, and awkwardly, he told me how he felt, I was astonished, and, although flattered and not a little amused, I realised that I needed to deal with this carefully.

I had to find a way not to hurt John's feelings and spoil the friendship we had. I thought rapidly and then told him that I was still very much it in love with Peter. Although I was fond of him as a friend that was as far as my relationship with him would go. He would, I knew, find a more suitable girl. Admittedly there weren't many girls in Bahrain but his time would come. His friendship, however, was important to all of us. We would not talk of this again.

One Life

He was quiet for a while then said he hoped I didn't dislike him now and left to return to the camp soon after. I told Peter about this and he laughed. Had I not noticed that he had the crush on me? He had! He said that he'd known I could handle it. I was a bit surprised at this, and not a little put out, although I was not quite sure why. Was he so sure of me? Peter never mentioned the incident again.

We had not been in Bahrain long before there was a complete money changeover from the rupee to the dinar, and we were given pamphlets about the new money. The changeover was made in one-day! It's amazing how quickly you learn these things when you have to.

On the day I was invited to the Sheik's palace with Jeanine, we were shown into a very large reception room dominated by a picture of him. There were lots of bedrooms and a huge kitchen with a big square cast-iron stove in the middle. The outside of the

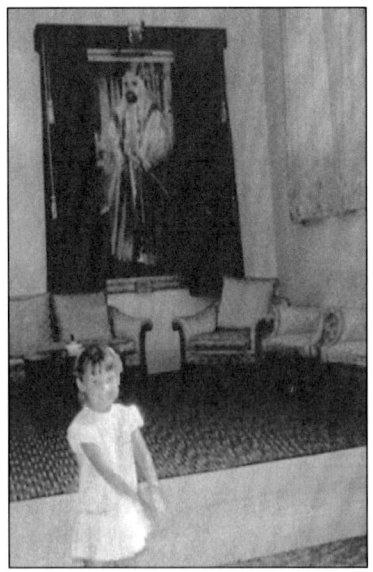

Jeanine in front of the Sheikh's portrait.

(Top) Outside the palace and (above) the reception room

Bahrain 1965

building was of an Arabian style and painted in a cool white. Unlike our Queen's palace in London there were no other portraits, paintings, pictures or furnishings, but there were beautiful sumptuous Persian carpets. A servant showed us a very large bathroom with a toilet, bidet and bath and then he proudly pointed to a large fridge at the end of the room! I had started to learn that different cultures held different values about what was important. After Jeanine had eaten her ice cream, and I had been served coffee, we left. I had enjoyed the visit; not everyone was invited to the palace.

The Sheikh certainly didn't lack for female company. The gossip was that service wives, Navy mostly, visited him regularly on their own, and, as a thank you for their favours, were given gold watches, though if found out they were also sent home. Peter told me that the Sheikh had joked with him that he liked his women with some meat on them, and that then, looking at me and laughing, he had dismissed me as too skinny! However, he did try to make amends by adding that he respected me as an intelligent woman and he enjoyed being with our family, especially the children who he allowed to go for short rides on his speed boat. I found him to be both a gentleman and interesting, as well as extremely knowledgeable. I have always taken people as I found them, and not as the local gossip would have them be.

Among the many places we visited whilst in Bahrain was a 16th century fort about which we were told stories by Arab friends. The story went that, many years ago, if an Arab committed a crime he was thrown off the tower. If he lived, he was not guilty, and if he died, he was guilty. There were also bullet holes in the walls where other offenders had been shot.

The women wore full purdah, black cloaks and face masks

One Life

which gave them the appearance of bat-like creatures. Their masks could range from head covering wrapped around their faces, to hideously ugly leather contraptions with only the eyes peering out from slits. These were enough to frighten anyone. Their cloaks, which often covered the most gorgeous dresses, covered more than just beautiful clothes. I was told this on a rare occasion when we were invited for a meal at a well-to-do Arab's house. I had my head, shoulders and arms covered with a large shawl, and, upon arrival at our host's house, had been warmly welcomed.

On entering we took off our shoes, as was the custom, and washed our feet before entering a reception room. Around the walls of this room were mattresses to sit on. This was an all-men affair, the women having their own room across the courtyard. The rooms were arranged around a square courtyard, with one room on each corner, and there was a courtyard in the middle.

As a privileged visitor, I was to stay with the men. It felt very strange and I would rather have stayed with the women. However there I was, sitting cross legged. I had no camera with me on this occasion. Plates of food were brought in and placed on cloths in the middle of round brass trays with ornate carved wooden feet. I knew that I must not use my right hand to take food as the right hand is considered unclean. The ensuing discussion (in English) was very male orientated. I was addressed on occasions and was asked if I enjoyed being in Bahrain. I then dared to ask, receiving a look of horror from Peter, if I may see the women. After a perplexed and shocked look from the men they conceded to my wish, one of the men first going to see the women – to warn them, I suppose. Then he came back to escort me across the courtyard.

It turned out to be well worth the risk of asking. I discovered

Bahrain 1965

that the woman were very powerful. Most spoke good English. In fact, two of them had been educated in England and one of their sons, the youngest child, was presently at Eton College.

The women talked freely to me about their culture, delighted that I had asked to spend time with them. They explained to me that Arab women enjoyed the anonymity wearing purdah gave them. It afforded them the ability to go wherever they chose, with neither husband nor other family members knowing who was behind the black robes. They also told me that it was they, and not their husbands, who were in control. Like many other truly clever woman before them, they just allowed their husbands to think they were in charge. It was necessary, they said, to feed their men's ego. I learned a good deal from these women. They had their own privacy within the marriage, their own rooms, and, although they knew their place within the marriage, they believed they were in full control and happy. I was to learn very much later that having your own space and identity within a marriage is not easy to achieve.

All too soon our two and a half years in Bahrain came to an end and we returned to England. What a time we had had and what a lot of wonderful memories we had to take back with us!

One Life

Chapter Eighteen

Naphill 1967: A New Baby and Betrayal

After the excitement and reunions on our return to England, and following another short transit stay in a house at RAF Warton, we moved to our new posting at Naphill. Naphill is near Walters Ash, Buckinghamshire and we found ourselves in an interesting old house with a large garden, situated on the main road near to the guardroom of the camp.

Peter was again away during the week inspecting camps throughout England and, although he returned each Friday, he was often on mess duty over the weekend, and so the children saw little of him. Even so, I was glad of the little time I did have with him, and he enjoyed these duties behind the bar.

Just as had been a problem previously, Paul found changing school again very stressful and never really settled. He came home despondent and, for the first time, did not want to go to school. I explained that this was not an option and pointed out the need for education and how much I had missed out on mine due to the war. I also told him that I could be put into prison if he didn't go to school!

Usually a very good child, this was the first sign of rebellion and unhappiness Paul had ever shown, and I really felt upset for him. Peter and I discussed boarding school. We knew that parting with our children for long spells would be an enormous wrench, and then there was the cost. However, I wanted the children to have what I had missed out on: a good steady schooling. There were grants available for service children's schooling where their education was being disrupted. We looked at schools whilst finding out about the cost and grant situation. In the meantime Paul became quiet and withdrawn, spending much time in his bedroom, reading.

At the parent's evening, a few weeks later, his teacher said that Paul was not taking part in the classroom activities and was not living up to the report from his last school in Bahrain. I assured her that he was doing his homework and had shown me his project on the liner *Queen Elizabeth II*. He had worked out the number of crew, and the costs, and the food needed, and had drawn a full sketch of the ship. We had even been to the library to research facts together.

His teacher was surprised saying that he certainly had not bought this to school and shared it with her. They had been doing a project at the school on this very subject. I said I would see that Paul brought it in and handed it to her. After seeing it, she said that it was obvious to her that changing schools had severely unsettled Paul, and that maybe he needed a more settled schooling at a boarding school.

Thankfully Andrew's teacher seemed happy with his progress and the friends he had already made, and told me that he had settled in quickly.

We were now looking seriously at boarding school education for both children. I did not want them to be separated and felt that both the boy's education would certainly suffer with the constant moves.

We enjoyed Friday evenings at the mess. These normally included a quiz and a couple of rounds of bingo before a fish-and-chip or pie-and-peas supper. It was there that we met and made friends with Lindsay and Norman who lived down the road from us. Lindsay had a part time job as a typist. Their two boys,

Naphill 1967: A New Baby and Betrayal

twelve and thirteen, were boarders at Scarisbrick Hall, Ormskirk. They could not, they said, praise the school enough. Their two boys had been at the school for two years now and were very happy there. We had become very despondent by this time, having already looked at five different boarding schools which had ranged from very poor to mediocre in standard. Often they had only a tarmac playground and, seemingly, there were no satisfactory hobbies run outside of the school hours. We'd looked at everything from the qualifications held by the teaching staff to the philosophy of the school. We had been just about to give up prior to this conversation with Lindsay and Norman.

They gave us a copy of the prospectus and we wrote off for up to date information and an appointment. We were impressed with the prospectus. It was not a glossy marketing affair but a small compact booklet full of information and photographs of the school. We took the opportunity to talk with Lindsay and Norman's two boys a couple of weeks later when they were on half-term break. We then visited the school, driving through open countryside and arriving at the ornate gates to the driveway that swept up to the impressive building.

Scarisbrick Hall is described as the finest example of Gothic Renaissance architecture in the country and is an officially listed building. On entering we found that the elaborate oak carvings, panelling and the exquisitely decorated ceilings, were overpowering in their beauty. We wondered if the rest would impress us as much and we were not to be disappointed.

We were able to speak freely with pupils at the school, and they appeared relaxed, one boy even telling us that he felt they should be allowed more television time and pocket money! Each pupil was allowed three shillings and six pence per week, irrespective of the parent's means, so that all pupils were equal,

One Life

and television was strictly limited and censored. The boys appeared proud of and happy at their school, always politely standing to one side to allow us to pass. The bedrooms were light and airy, with the patterned curtains a contrast to the ornate oak panelling. A teddy bear lay on one small boy's bed.

We spoke with the matron, who was a kindly (not at all starched), motherly person, and said that bed wetting wasn't a problem and, if it did occur, was dealt with very sympathetically and quietly so as not to embarrass the child. Fortunately my boys did not have this problem, but we felt it an example of the school's caring attitude.

Then we looked at the class, science and common rooms and the modern gymnasium. Voluntary activities included badminton, cycling, canoeing, riding, photography, wood work, metalwork and automobile engineering. For sports the boys played soccer and cricket. Fixtures were arranged with other schools including representation at the annual sports day of the Independent Schools Association. The boys had comfortable common rooms, with magazines, record players and pianos, a large games room with table tennis, and a TV room. We were invited to take afternoon tea with the staff and talked with the form-masters, house-masters and the headmaster.

After tea we took a stroll around the surrounding 38 acre estate with its woodland, delightful gardens, orchard and lake, which all combined to give the school an air of freedom. The coast resort and shopping centre of Southport was only four miles distant. Scarisbrick Hall had been purchased by the headmaster, Mr. Oxley, an honours graduate in Hebrew and Bible Studies, for the purpose of establishing a school with accommodation for 140 boys from the age of eight upwards. Pupils from the age of eleven had to pass an entrance exam.

Naphill 1967: A New Baby and Betrayal

Not only were we were looking at the school's educational success, but also its atmosphere, ethos, social activities and Christian background, and we believed that we had found what we were looking for.

We had a holiday together before the boys started boarding school and hired a boat on the River Thames. The children were all good swimmers and we went up river to Chertsey, visiting Hampton Court and other places on route. This was the early season; we could not be guaranteed good weather and so took wellington boots and duffel coats. Fortunately our boat was very cosy and warm.

It was all great fun. The boys loved helping their dad with the boat, particularly when going through the many locks, and we needed this time together as a family. Waking to the gentle rocking movement of the boat, the ducks quacking, birds singing, and the gentle lapping of the water against the side of the boat was an experience not to be missed. The peace and the slow pace of life, the friendly greetings from passing boat owners, and pulling together as a family, all added to a successful holiday which we all enjoyed.

The boys had both passed the entrance exam and were now about to start their first term at boarding school. Getting them ready took a lot of organisation. The initial costs were high: they needed an expensive trunk to last their time through school, and school uniforms with six of everything. I sold my jewellery, and the expensive hi-fi we had bought ourselves in Bahrain. We labelled every item as instructed.

Both boys appeared happy and excited at starting at boarding school. I'm sure that their having met and spent time with Lindsay and Norman's two sons made a great difference. The four of them would be going after the Christmas break and both

One Life

sets of parents and the four children arrived together, their trunks fastened onto our cars' roof racks. We left after seeing them settled into their respective rooms, each boy sharing with three others. I managed to keep back my tears for the boys' sakes, until we were back in the car and on our way home.

After their half term break at home, we saw them back to school on the train from London. They would be met from the train at the other end. Lindsay and I developed a ritual. We would see the boys off, hiding our tears, and then go shopping in London and have tea before returning home. I suppose this would be called retail therapy now. I always hated seeing my two boys off to school. The boys did write letters home, though this task appeared to be mostly delegated to Paul, being the eldest.

Jeanine attended Naphill Walters Ash Co-Educational School for four to eleven year olds. She appeared happy at school, was progressing well, and now, at nearly eight years old, she joined the local Brownie pack. I was, of course, very happy about her joining. Having been a Brownie and Guide myself, I knew the value of being part of the Guiding movement.

We looked at boarding education for Jeanine, looking at residential ballet schools. She took the entrance exam to one of the best, near London, and passed. However, I felt that she was still too young, and anyway, her enjoyment of ballet seemed to be giving way to her love of Brownies. Was I perhaps trying to impose my ideas on her? Could I really part with her? Could I cope with all my children away at boarding school at opposite ends of the country? We decided not, and besides which, there was no grant for schooling until a child reached the age of eleven years. Looking at the financial strain that this would also impose on us, we decide not to send Jeanine into boarding school at this time.

Jeanine's best friend went to the Brownie Pack with her, and

Naphill 1967: A New Baby and Betrayal

the meetings were held in a hut just inside the main camp gates. She had been attending for just a few weeks when I was asked to help, as their Brown Owl desperately needed assistance. I was missing the boys and had time on my hands, so agreed. Thus I was back in the world of Guiding, this time as an adult. I soon felt that I had never been away, settling in and becoming very involved.

Jeanine flourished: she was enrolled in the June of 1967 and soon gained her Animal Lover's Badge and her Gold Bar test. Somehow we managed to keep the space between my being her mother as well as her 'Snowy Owl' at the Brownie pack. Brown Owl was an inspiration to everyone. I attended meetings with her at the District Commissioner's house. The Guide Commissioner in charge in our area was also a real gem, encouraging everyone in the area to develop the youngsters in their packs. I gained my Assistant Brownie Guider warrant in January 1968 for the First Water's Ash Pack. I loved working with the Brownie Guides, this age group was a joy! The little girls, their faces shining, were so eager to learn, and wore their Brownie uniform with such pride.

As I had found with my boys, from the ages of 7 to 10 years a child has an open and inquisitive mind and soaks up knowledge like a sponge; they are fresh, eager and trusting. This puts a great deal of responsibility upon all who have been given the privilege of being involved, in whatever small way, in their development. The Brownies give these children an outlet for their enthusiasm, imagination, teamwork and boundless energy. We had visits to places of interest, badges to work for, kerb-drill, and first aid. Then there was 'Thinking Day' when we all thought about other Brownies in countries where they had much less than we had. The Brownies also learned where key local places were, such as

One Life

at the post office and police station. Enrolment was an important event for a new Brownie: when each one would solemnly say: 'I promise to do my best.'

I am sure that Peter being away during the week, both when we were in England and sometimes when abroad, helped to keep our marriage alive. Out of our twenty-two year service life, well over half of it was spent apart. So reunions were exciting, rekindling our love for each other on a regular basis.

Despite this, and although I couldn't see it happening for many years, I looked forward to the day when Peter would not always be going away. He loved the service life, especially its mixture of independence and travelling, and the job satisfaction it gave him. If only subconsciously, I feel that he also liked the feeling of security, of being looked after, that being a member of the services gave him. Housing was supplied, there were no worries about where to live, and a regular wage coming in. In addition, marching in and out of married quarters was wholly my responsibility, as were the children. So, all in all, it seemed to be a pretty good life for the service man!

Nevertheless, the two and a half year retirement posting (usually in the UK) that servicemen received, after twenty-two years or more, did not really prepare them for civilian life. The wife, on the other hand, had to become more confident and self reliant if the marriage was not to fail through loneliness, the constant moving about, the missing out on all 'family back home' contact, and the impossibility of putting down roots. And then, of course, there was the disruptive effect on the children's education and, for some, the difficulty in making new friends and the lack of any real opportunities to further their own careers.

I was lucky for, apart from loneliness, and the breakdown I had now recovered from, I loved travelling. I had been an

Naphill 1967: A New Baby and Betrayal

independent person for most of my life. This had all started with my wartime evacuation and having to fend for myself as a child. To coin a modern phrase, I felt I was street wise, and I had no immediate family ties, though sometimes I believed this to be a mixed blessing! Moving and travelling started very early in my life and I enjoyed being a service wife.

I was also now working part time at Storey's, a furnishing firm, where I typed invoices, did the filing, and answered the phone. My typing was getting better and this work experience was to help me when I eventually settled after coming out of the services.

Then I thought I'd got flu, and when I did not recover as soon as expected, I went to see the doctor. I was experiencing uneasy gastric feelings. In a way I was quite right, for, after examining me, the doctor laughed and declared, 'You are at least seven months pregnant. How can you have missed the signs?'

Not having missed a period I was very shocked and surprised.

The doctor added that although the baby was very small it was fully formed: 'I will give you a course of vitamins,' he said: 'and arrange some blood tests and a clinic appointment for you. I'd love to see your husband's face when you tell him!'

He said he knew Peter well as they were both members of the same medical team.

I didn't know what to think. My mind was in a whirl. By now I'd been working at Storey's for some time and was enjoying the job. The money came in very handy as we had Andrew's fees to pay because the service would not contribute until he was over eleven years. Even though I'd begun to look forward to the birth of this baby (at the age of thirty-three I was feeling much more mature), I would have to stop work. When Peter returned on the

One Life

Friday he was very shocked. He also had news of his own: we were to be posted to Singapore.

I gave up work a couple of weeks later and each Wednesday, on her afternoon off, I went with Lindsay to town, shopping for the new baby. And, on a hot, sunny 4th of July, Darren, our fourth child, made his appearance. At 4lb 6oz, he was small but healthy. Peter, who was away again doing his job, hurried back to see us both. Jeanine was being looked after by Lindsay and Norman, and Peter picked her up after visiting me in hospital.

Little did I know then that Peter was having an affair with Lindsay. I only found out after my second admission to hospital when Darren was eight weeks old. I'd eaten some egg-yolk, whilst feeding Darren, and the consequent massive reaction catapulted me into a migraine. I also got a rash all over my body. I was in hospital for 48 hours being given injections and a good telling off. I have never been tempted to eat eggs again.

Soon after arriving back home, I was sitting outside in the garden when my next-door neighbour came round to look at my new baby. Quietly, she told me that I ought to be aware of the goings-on between my so-called friend and my husband. She said that normally she would have kept this to herself, but she knew I was well liked by those around me and therefore felt that I should know about it so that I could do something before they found out. I was all set to make an angry retort but then I saw the look of genuine concern on her face. She added that she'd seen them kissing as Lindsay had left my house late one evening whilst I was in hospital.

'They were so engrossed in each other,' she said, 'that they didn't even notice us going past on our way home from the mess.'

I stared at her in dismay. 'Are you sure?' I whispered.

Naphill 1967: A New Baby and Betrayal

Again she said that she was very sorry, and left hastily.

I sat down. At first I was just stunned and disbelieving. I felt as though my guts had been torn out. It couldn't be true. She must be mistaken.

I challenged Peter as soon as he arrived home and knew immediately that something was very wrong by his sheepish attitude. When I said I was going to talk with Lindsay, and then Norman, he became decidedly upset.

He said, 'It didn't mean anything. It was only a fleeting affair. She's been very unhappy and I was only comforting her when it happened. I love you and nobody else. After all, we're being posted. I'll be gone in a fortnight's time.'

My mind was racing. What was I to do? I was devastated, loving him as I did, and now we had a new baby. I looked at him in despair. Then, disgusted, I turned and walked out of the house. It was seven in the evening, still hot and sultry. He tried to follow me.

'Go back,' I said, 'and look after your son and daughter, I want to think.'

I walked and walked, feeling numb and flat.

What?

Why?

How?

What had I done to make him look at Lindsay?

What had Lindsay got that I hadn't?

What about Norman? Did he know?

I thought about Peter, what we had been through, and the fun that we had enjoyed in Bahrain. Was this really just a one-off as he had declared? He did look devastated, but then he would do wouldn't he? What was I going to do? If I left him, where would I go? I had no money, no home, and no job. And now I had four

223

One Life

children. How would they react? I found myself in front of Lindsay's quarter. Should I confront her? Should I speak to Norman? What a mess!

I walked up the path lifted my hand to the knocker, and when the door opened, there was Lindsay, the welcome in her eyes fading as they looked into mine:

'You know?' she whispered.

'Yes,' I said. 'How could you? You were my friend.'

She stepped out, pulling the door shut behind her.

'Can we talk away from the house?' she whispered, 'Norman must not find out.'

'Now,' I said firmly, 'let's walk.'

She went back in, returning quickly, and looking pale and agitated. I do not know what she said to Norman. We walked for some distance in silence.

Then I said just one little word: 'Why?'

'I don't know,' she said. 'It just happened. Norman and I had just had a massive row. He'd hit me and then marched out leaving me in tears. The children and Jeanine were in bed. Then Peter arrived and I was crying. He just put his arm around me, consoling me.'

'You did not have to carry on with the affair,' I said.

'I know,' she said miserably, 'but my marriage is going through a really bad stage. It was the comfort. Peter said he didn't love me. He said he adored you, and that he always would. I'm so sorry. Norman and I have sorted out our differences and, in a way this has helped me to see what I actually wanted. I'm really sorry. I don't want my marriage to break-up. Please don't tell Norman…'

'Oh go on home,' I said.

Naphill 1967: A New Baby and Betrayal

For some time I just kept walking, trying to think clearly about the future, but all I could think of was that, following baby Darren's christening in two weeks time, Peter was going to Singapore. I still loved him, and with this thought in my mind I started to walk back home to my family.

I arrived back at the house feeling calm, yet feeling numb. Then, on going in, the first thing I saw was Peter with Darren in his arms, walking up and down, gently trying to quieten our baby's sobs as his own tears ran down his face. The picture this presented to me brought a tender forgiveness within my broken heart.

I made a cup of tea, and, taking it through to the sitting room, sat down in quiet reflection. Peter settled Darren down in his cot to sleep and then he sat down opposite me.

'What are you going to do?' he said.

We talked at length about the events of the past weeks and eventually agreed to put them behind us. We were not to mention the subject again unless another, more serious, crisis arose.

Darren's christening had now been arranged and we decided that it should go ahead; we did not wish Norman to find out through us, and I didn't wish him to suffer as I had. Although tensions were obviously present, we carried on with the ceremony. The boys were to be the godfathers. My reasoning for this being that often older godparents either died, or lost touch, probably just when their support and guidance was needed most.

The christening was held on Paul's birthday, 25th August 1968. I felt that the boys would fulfil the godfather roles probably better than most. They would later show their commitment when Darren hit a crisis in his life. I made a christening gown of silk and lace. The Brownies, who loved Darren to bits, were of course part of the christening, and appear in a photo at the church door

One Life

with Brown Owl and me. Everyone wanted to hold Darren, including Jeanine, who smothered rather than mothered him. Peter set off for Singapore the following week, leaving me to pack, hand over the quarter, and follow with Jeanine and baby Darren in a few weeks time.

Peter's parents couldn't come for the christening, but came soon after, before we left for Singapore. Dad brought his guide dog. I now had plenty of room in the house for the five of us and the dog. We had picnics and spent a lot of time in the garden. I really enjoyed their stay, and they had time to enjoy their fourth grandchild before setting off home.

I'd begun to pack and prepare to join Peter when I learned I was to be given a surprise present from the CO as a thank you for my work with the Brownies. I couldn't believe it! I was allocated an airman to help with the packing up and handing over of the married quarter, and we were all to be driven in the CO's staff car all the way to the airport. What a wonderful way to be thanked for doing something I'd loved doing!

I also received a letter from Peter saying the CO at RAF Seletar had asked if I would be Guide Commissioner for the Singapore North Guides and Brownies when I arrived in Singapore. This job was usually carried out by the CO's wife. However, they'd wanted someone who was a Guider and knew about Guiding. Apparently, I'd been recommended by my guide commissioner at Walter's Ash. I was honoured to be asked, albeit a little scared of the responsibility. I would have to lead a number of Guide and Brownie packs, their leaders being of different nationalities and cultures. And, I'd not only be representing the Guiding movement, but also the Services. I thought hard about what a challenge it would be.

In his letter, Peter said that the CO's wife had offered her

Naphill 1967: A New Baby and Betrayal

house for the meetings as ours would not be large enough. I would also be given full support. By now I'd been told that, when last year I had been sent on a Commissioners Conference, my own Commissioner, and Brown Owl, had both given me glowing references. After talking with my Commissioner, who said she had every faith in my abilities, I accepted. Then I said a sad farewell to Brown Owl and the Brownies, and left with the precious little gifts they had given to me so lovingly. I would miss them greatly.

Packing up and moving was, by now, a smooth operation. Darren was a very good baby, sleeping through the night and happily gurgling to himself through the day.

I left on a high, looking forward to, if a little scared of, the responsibility I was about to take on. Once again there was the excitement of a new country and culture to explore.

I settled down comfortably for the very long flight to Singapore.

One Life

Chapter Nineteen

Singapore 1968

The first thing I noticed on descending from the aircraft in Singapore was the oppressive humidity. It was like walking into the steam from a kettle and not at all like the dry arid heat had I experienced in Bahrain a few years before. There was also much more greenery. Rubber trees lined the route from the airport and I learned that they were tapped, and the latex collected, mid-morning. Our flat, in the village of Jalan Kyu, was not far from the RAF camp. We would only be here a short while as I would need to live on camp to enable me to carry out my role as Guide Commissioner.

We rested before setting off to the night markets. In Singapore work started very early in the day and stopped in the early afternoon, the place came alive again in the cooler evenings. People took things easy in the heat of the day. It was siesta time. Whilst I rested, I read a little about this country I was to live in for two and a half years.

Singapore Island is at the southern tip of the Malay Peninsula. It is known as Lion City and was established as one of the world's first

Latex collection from rubber trees.

One Life

ports, becoming a centre for the rubber, pepper, and tin trades. It was early in the 19th century that Sir Stamford Raffles of the East India Company first created a trading station from marsh, jungle and a scattered melee of kampongs.

After our rest we took a trishaw to the main markets and into the pulsating oriental world of Singapore. On the way, we were fascinated by the lantern makers, we met fortune-telling birds with their sages, and were intrigued by the herbalists who sold delicately scented drinks. There were also men from Nepal and Burma selling precious stones, and fruit stalls full of the bright and appetising produce of the tropics.

We got off our trishaw in Chinatown, a crowded area, and the night air was now filled with the babble of a thousand Asian dialects. The crashing of gongs and cymbals made me jump and the air was heavy with the enticing aromas from countless food stalls. It seemed that wherever I looked there were more visual delights and I felt dizzy from the night's heavy mixture of unbelievably bright colours and sultry seductive sounds. The excitement of these night markets would linger forever in my memory.

Tired but happy, and after doing some initial shopping and eating our first Chinese meal at a spotlessly clean stall, we returned to our flat. Jeanine and Darren fell asleep quickly, and at last Peter and I had time for each other. We soon settled down and I wrote to our two older boys back in England to tell them a little about the journey and Singapore.

I explored Jalan Kyu which consisted of a row of shops each side of the dusty road leading on to the RAF base. There was a friendly atmosphere and a small food stall that came alive at night. I ate here often in the coming years, usually after late rehearsals at the theatre club.

Singapore 1968

Singapore was remarkably clean and the people were healthy, energetic and happy. Their multi-coloured washing, strung out on long bamboo poles, looked for all the world like the banners of some vast army. At that time, the Malay's, Indians, and Pakistanis worked together successfully, forming a highly sophisticated community of people who were proudly loyal, despite their varied racial origins.

The Chinese New Year was a bright, noisy, cheerful occasion. Everyone dressed in fine, new clothes and there were firecrackers, lion dances, and family celebrations. And for Diwali, the Hindu festival of light, people celebrated by surrounding their houses with lighted wicks in saucers of oil which flickered and glowed all through the long, hot, tropical night.

We soon moved onto the camp and settled down to life in Singapore. I enjoyed the theatre club activities, and produced a one act play. These plays were not only for entertainment but also to find a person able to produce or direct the next play for public performance. When the main play was being cast, others in the club would also make their own cast list. The person getting nearest to the producer's own casting would win a prize and be recognised as a possible producer for the next big production. Of course the prize

Peter and me at a Sergeants' Mess Dinner

One Life

winner would also need to have a good track record in the theatre. In practice the opportunity to actually produce and direct came rarely, as there were always very experienced and well known contenders in the field, so I had no expectations. Imagine my surprise, then, when I won the casting draw and produced a one act play called *Profile*, by T. C. Thomas, which received a good adjudication.

Here I am on the right talking with a guide when on visit to Malaysia.

1968-69 turned out to be very busy. In my role as Guide Commissioner, I was visiting Guide and Brownie packs in the North Division. I had a multicultural team of Guiders; English, Singaporean, Malaysian and Australian, who all ran Rangers,

Singapore 1968

Guides, and Brownie packs. All Singapore school children at that time had to belong to a youth club of some kind and the teachers in schools had to run them.

At the next guiders meeting it was decided that we should put on a show to make some money for charity and, at the same time, enable the Rangers, Guides and Brownies to obtain certain badges. It fell to me to ask the base's Commanding Officer, and President of the Theatre Club, if we could use the theatre, together with the services of the technicians and stage manager.

This theatre club was one of the best anywhere, with its stage, auditorium, lighting-box, dressing-room, props-room, ticket office and, of course, a bar and club room. This last, open all day and late into the evening, was run by a young Chinese barman who would cook snack meals whenever requested. I spent a good deal of my time in the theatre club getting ready for the Guide's forthcoming review *Beginners Please*.

The drama group was held next door to the church. The padre, with whom I became friendly, would jump over the monsoon drain running between the Theatre Club and the church, sit down at the club piano, and pound out vigourous music. I always assumed that this was after he'd had a difficult session with someone. He was great fun and gave me a good perspective on religion and the other service padres. I was also encouraged to join the choir and Jeanine joined me soon afterwards. Then, after doing the make-up for them, I was asked to join the Choral Society and accepted.

Darren was now toddling and was very fond of throwing toys into the deep monsoon drain flowing through our garden. We had to cover it over with something in order to keep him and his toys safe. Darren also spent a good deal of time with me in the Theatre club and he loved Ruby, our amah (maid), who adored him. Ruby had her own room and facilities at the end of our garden, accommodation which was highly prized by amah's working for service personnel. She was just sixteen years old when she started work for us, and I taught her English. She also learned alongside Darren as he began to chatter energetically. I gradually trusted her with him, and Jeanine who was a rascal of a child and up to everything. Jeanine played tricks on her at times, and there appeared to be a mutual testing out of the rules between them.

And so, back to the review *Beginners Please*. Since I was in the Theatre Club, it was suggested that I direct and produce the review. We had rehearsals and preparations well in hand. It was an opportunity for everyone to experience being in a production in a real theatre, and they all put in a tremendous amount of hard work to ensure a successful show. The Guiders each taught their

The Rangers on stage in Player Queen

Singapore 1968

packs individually and I called in from time to time to see how they were getting on. This was more for encouragement than anything else. I then put the show together and also produced a play with the Ranger Guides called *Player Queen* by Kathleen Stafford. This photograph shows the Rangers on stage in their costumes, the Queen, fifth from the left, gained her speech and drama award for her speech in the play.

Described as an imaginary incident, *Player Queen* is a delightful glimpse of what might have happened one June evening in 1602 at the court of Queen Elizabeth I. Our

The Brownie Play. Here I have been presented with flowers by the cast of Beginners Please.

(Right) The Queen, fifth from the left

One Life

production was reviewed by John Bates who was very complimentary, and in conclusion wrote:

> The full houses to which the show played should have helped a great deal with funding and the talent displayed on stage convinced me that all the Rangers, Guides and Brownies taking part thoroughly deserve the badges they will obtain. In short, the show was a great credit to all who acted, helped, produced, and directed it.'

From the proceeds we were also able to equip a home for the handicapped with bedspreads, and then adopted this home for our yearly charity.

Soon after this I was invited to the Istana, the official residence and office of the President of Singapore, for a Guide celebration dinner. The year was rounded off with pantomimes, Choral Society shows, and mess Christmas dos and dances. I was having a wonderful time.

The following year, 1970, was to be even better and started off with a surprise present given to Peter and me from the CO in recognition of all our efforts in 1969. It turned out to be a wonderful holiday in the Cameron Highlands in Malaysia. What could be better than being thanked so magnificently for what I loved doing!

We spent our holiday at Tana Ratah, a town in the cool and picturesque mountains, and stayed in the old smokehouse which has been a hotel since the highland's earliest colonial days. The town was always a popular hill station refuge for us British and has a very English atmosphere with its Tudor-style buildings, cottage gardens, log fires and roast beef dinners. Lured by the cool climate, people came here for a respite from the heat of

Singapore 1968

Aborigine with blowpipe.

Tea picking.

Singapore and a taste of home, though getting there involved a long trek up twisting, narrow mountain passes. Mist shrouded lush green rain forests swathe the highlands which are a two hour drive from Kuala Lumpur.

Amongst our other experiences of local life, we discovered

Peter with Darren and Jeanine.

Me, on a climb through the jungle.

how the indigenous people were lured into making an appearance by bribes of cigarettes, would show us how they used their blow pipes. These were 8 feet long and made of a type of bamboo only obtainable in this part of Malaysia. The poison for the dart tips was also obtained from local plants.

Singapore 1968

Later we watched the tea being picked from the row upon row of manicured bushes which carpet the hills and look very much like our own native privet hedges. Finally, and feeling very much refreshed after our holiday, we arrived back in Singapore.

As 1970 was diamond jubilee year for the Girl Guides Association, we decided that we should do something special to recognise this. We all agreed that the RAF Seletar would provide a perfect venue and that I'd write a letter to the CO asking his permission to use the camp facilities. In the meantime we'd do some planning and draw up a list of events.

We soon realised we would need to have events for all ages. These would include track and field athletics, obstacle races, gymnastics, and a test course to examine everyone on first aid, knots, the use of the compass, and their knowledge of Singapore. The guides would even provide a flagpole erection team. We made a list of dignitaries and guests to invite and thus everyone

Singapore Girl Guides Association
North Division

1910 - Diamond Jubilee - 1970
of the Guide Movement

SPORTS & FIELD DAY
RAF SELETAR
20 JUNE 1970

By Kind Permission of Group Captain A. Maisner, CBE AFC RAF

I join in Brownie revels.

The Programme.

One Life

was catered for, although the detailed planning would take several weeks. All these arrangements had to be laid out clearly for the CO with the request, as very strict rules had to be adhered to by those using RAF premises. Fortunately the CO said he was delighted to give us his permission and the date was fixed for the 27th of June 1970 which was just three months ahead.

As the preparation time passed I soon found that I needed to be in several places at once. Everyday someone would come to me for information and direction and I learned a great deal in the process. Peter was always somewhere doing something towards the event. We were both far too busy to have personal problems.

I seemed to visit everywhere, encouraging the pack leaders and the multitude of Guides and Brownies involved. Eventually the great day dawned, and thankfully all the planning and organisation paid off. Bus loads of children arrived, followed by the honoured guests. We all had a wonderful time. So many people had all come together to make this very special Diamond Jubilee such a stunning success.

How lucky I was to have been involved! And what a fantastic amount I had learned! Teamwork, and, above all, appreciating each other's efforts helped so much in making things happen. This was to help me much later when working in a team outside of the services. I still treasure the letter I received from the Divisional Commissioner after the event saying that she felt the way Peter and I worked together was a credit and example to others.

At the next Guiders meeting it was decided that, since the services were pulling out of Singapore at the end of the year, this would be the last opportunity for the Guides and Scouts to visit Kuala Lumpur in Malaysia, so a visit was arranged.

Singapore 1968

Once again there was much to be done. Peter accompanied us as a service representative and together we wrote a piece for the camp magazine. The following is a short excerpt:

To Kuala Lumpur – site-seeing – August 1970

A two day site seeing trip to Kuala Lumpur: simple: with fifty Guides and Scouts?! I don't think so. We needed passports, permits, inoculations, vaccinations, and insurance. It was, forms and yet more forms! What age are the children? Who is in charge? What language do they speak? Have they got travel documents? Yes, madam, but, having got them into Malaysia, can you get them out again? What about Molly's headache pills? Blimey! Would it never end?

Eventually it did! On 10th August, 25 Guides and Scouts and seven Guiders and Scouters assembled at the guide hut. Brian Dee hadn't got his cholera certificate – 'Go and get it lad!' Where was the bus? Sterling work by the Group Scout Leader and a willing parent eventually produced the bus and the party enjoyed a swift run into Singapore.

Keppel station: now the District Commissioner had to try to explain to a perplexed customs official that: 'these children are all with me but they are not my children.' Then to our sleeper, only to find, a bit like Goldilocks, that someone has not just been sleeping in our beds, but was still there! Fortunately we find there's been a last minute switch round. We are in coach O, and not S, and finally we all do get a bunk.

Now we're off! Immigration at the causeway is very pleasant and efficient – thanks to the letter we are carrying which is covered in impressive official seals. Gradually everyone quietens down and even manage to sleep through the brightly moonlit

One Life

Malaysian night. How do I know this? Well, because I was awake of course!

It is 7.30 a.m.. The heat of the day has still to arrive and it feels cool and crisp. Kuala Lumpur has one of Asia's finest railway stations and its minarets are shining pink in the early morning sunlight. Even the sleepiest amongst us are struck by its beauty.

Breakfast at the station buffet: the manager must have thought I was mad when I walked in alone, and ordered 14 teas, 18 coffees, and 32 scrambled eggs on toast. Maybe, or maybe not, he is relieved when, a few minutes later, our party of the 32 arrives. The meal over, well fed and rested, we make our way to our hotels: then, after showers and a change of clothes, we are ready for the off.

We visit the Lake Gardens and the National Museum and then everyone is hungry again and it's time to find a restaurant. Is it 10 curried chickens, 15 bowls of fried rice and seven ham salads or was it seven curried chicken, and ten bowls of fried rice? Well eventually it is all sorted out and about an hour later 25 tired children, and their equally tired escorts, are reclining peacefully in the YMCA lounge: for all of about five minutes: how do they recover so quickly?

The afternoon begins with a visit to the National Mosque. The Guiders and Ian (who would have to wear short shorts) are now draped with black cloaks – rather like bats A rather ancient Chinese temple is our next stop, then on to the Merdeka (marking the day Malaya became independent from the UK in 1957) Stadium. Before us is a magnificent running track. It is 3.30 p.m. and the temperature is in the 80s. What a challenge! Some resist the temptation but half of our party, including the commissioner, run a full lap cheered on by the rest, a crowd of workmen and

Singapore 1968

some very bemused security guards. The commissioner comes in sixth!

Now, and after a well earned cold drink, we are making our way slowly through the streets of KL's Chinatown to the rendezvous restaurant where the head waiter is overheard to say to the commissioner: 'We welcome you and your children, Madame, but you have caused great confusion in my cook.' After an excellent meal we head back to our hotels. It is at this point that Jim disappears; something is afoot!

Next morning the secret's out! Somehow the Scouts have discovered that today is the commissioner's birthday and we're all awakened at 7 a.m. by a rousing chorus of *Happy Birthday*. The resultant party only breaks up after very sleepy commissioner cuts the magnificent cake which Jim had only obtained after an exhaustive tour of the local bakeries.

Today's a day for conducted sightseeing tours. Our comfortable bus takes us all around Kuala Lumpur then out to explore every corner of the limestone Batu Caves which are regarded with great reverence by the Hindu people; of especial interest is the sacred five-legged cow. A cold drink and then its off to a tin mine, where everyone leaves with small samples.

There's just time for last-minute souvenir buying before meeting up at the hotel for our big feast. Who says children don't like Chinese food? Soon we are chop-sticking our way through eight delicious courses. There's much laughter at our efforts to use the sticks but nobody goes hungry. The meal over, we entertain our fellow diners with a selection of campfire songs and are rewarded by enthusiastic rounds of applause.

Tired but very happy we made our way back to the station and soon we are back at RAF Seletar with all our very many happy memories of a very successful trip.

One Life

Life seemed to be just one long whirl and, what with my roles in Guiding, the Theatre Club, the Church Choir and the Choral Society there never seemed enough time in the day. I had become known as 'Midge', my nick-name in the theatre club, which was useful in keeping my involvement in the theatre club and the

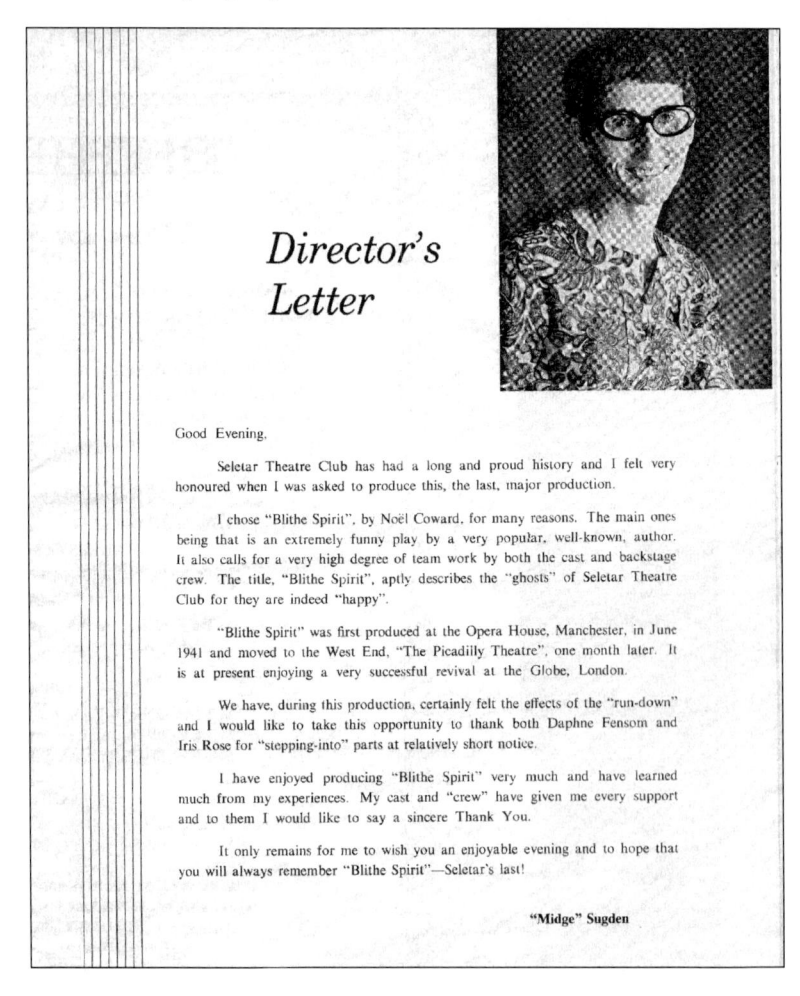

Director's Letter

Good Evening,

Seletar Theatre Club has had a long and proud history and I felt very honoured when I was asked to produce this, the last, major production.

I chose "Blithe Spirit", by Noël Coward, for many reasons. The main ones being that it is an extremely funny play by a very popular, well-known, author. It also calls for a very high degree of team work by both the cast and backstage crew. The title, "Blithe Spirit", aptly describes the "ghosts" of Seletar Theatre Club for they are indeed "happy".

"Blithe Spirit" was first produced at the Opera House, Manchester, in June 1941 and moved to the West End, "The Picadilly Theatre", one month later. It is at present enjoying a very successful revival at the Globe, London.

We have, during this production, certainly felt the effects of the "run-down" and I would like to take this opportunity to thank both Daphne Fensom and Iris Rose for "stepping-into" parts at relatively short notice.

I have enjoyed producing "Blithe Spirit" very much and have learned much from my experiences. My cast and "crew" have given me every support and to them I would like to say a sincere Thank You.

It only remains for me to wish you an enjoyable evening and to hope that you will always remember "Blithe Spirit"—Seletar's last!

"Midge" Sugden

My Director's letter from the programme with photo of me.

244

Singapore 1968

Guides separate. As Jeanine was herself involved in Brownies, dancing, and Sports Day competitions, we tried to keep it a secret that I was her mother in order to give her the freedom to enter these things. I made sure that I was not involved in choosing the winners! Jeanine addressed me as everyone else did, and it appeared to work.

I was now very busy directing and producing *Blithe Spirit*, our last big production before pulling out of Singapore. Rehearsals had started in earnest and everyone was working hard. Peter became the production co-ordinator, and I had a good stage manager in Lofty Bateman who ensured that all the special effects were extremely well done. On cue, ornaments would shoot off shelves and fly across rooms.

We waited nervously for the reviews. Amongst others, the *Singapore Herald*, the most popular paper, gave us a good write up and after that we performed to full houses. The play was a great success and what a joy and pleasure it was, when, on the last night, I was called on stage to be given flowers and presents. We had a great 'after the pay' do ending up on Mount Faber in the early morning, breakfast at Raffles, and drinking Singapore Slings to round off the whole marvellous experience.

My Guiding too was rounded off well when the Guides, Rangers, Brownies and Scouts held a goodbye bonfire in my honour.

Only one incident spoilt my stay in Singapore. I'd kept mostly healthy apart from a very few migraines, only one of which led to a fit. I wore my dark glasses on most occasions: they were part of me now. The boys were enjoying boarding school and came out to us for their long holidays. We took them around Singapore, showing them the sights and, being scouts, they joined us on the trip to Kuala Lumpur.

One Life

Life with Peter had its ups and downs, as with all marriages. On the whole, he was a loving caring person but his weakness for drink and women did mar our marriage.

Not long before returning home, Peter left for work with his usual parting: 'See you lunch time.' When he had not arrived by late evening I began to wonder where he was and called in at the Theatre Club, thinking he may have dropped in for a drink. At that moment the padre entered. He looked surprised when I asked him if he had seen Peter and said, 'Peter has gone on an exercise in the jungle for two weeks – hasn't he told you?'

I was devastated, but managed to keep my feelings in control until I got back home. Peter had left without telling me anything. How could he do this? How was I going to manage without house-keeping money for a fortnight? And why on earth had he done this?

The next day I asked Ruby, our amah, to bring in a tray of tea and cakes for my friend Brenda and me. As Ruby put the tray down, she burst into tears saying she was so ashamed. She was having a baby and that the baby was 'the master's' – in other words, Peter's.

'I am so sorry,' she whimpered, 'I have shamed my family.'

Then she told me that her family had found her a husband, an older man, who was willing to take her as his wife and to accept the baby.

I looked at her, finding it hard to believe. I felt as if my guts had been ripped out. She ran out and down the garden to her room, I looked after her, pityingly, feeling only sorrow and shame for her, and disgust for Peter. Not only had he again betrayed me but he had taken advantage of his position as her 'master' and then gone off leaving me to cope with his mess on my own. Brenda was looking at me; she too was shocked and lost for

Singapore 1968

words. Fortunately, not only did she comfort me, but I knew she would keep the knowledge to herself.

We talked at some length, deciding what was best to do. Then I went to Ruby and told her to go home and stay with her parents and that she would be looked after. Soon after this the Padre came to tell me that Peter had been flown back to hospital from the jungle as he had had an accident. Apparently he'd poured boiling water from a kettle onto his foot. It was not serious but he would be kept as an inpatient for a while. Nothing was ever said about the incident. However, his recent request to stay on in the service until fifty-five was turned down.

When Peter came home he was very subdued and denied everything that Ruby had said. I was emotionally drained and, though I told him how I felt, I had the children to think about. Since nothing had been said officially to me, and as we were leaving for England in a couple of days, I added that I believed it better for all concerned if I kept my own counsel.

As a service wife I couldn't just leave him. Not only were there the four children to consider but, as was normal in the services in those days, Peter had complete control of the finances. Wives didn't have bank accounts and so the family allowance was paid to the husband when abroad. Moving around, as we did, I could not have a settled career and I had no family. I was hardly going to go to the in-laws. I still loved Peter but I felt my respect for him was gradually disappearing.

By now everything, including all our boxes, had been packed and I had to buy an extra case for all the presents I'd received from so many people. I only hoped I would be

One Life

able to get them all through customs as they held such a lot of happy memories for me

My spirits were lifted by receiving the following thank you letter from the Commanding Officer of the camp.

From: Group Captain A. MAISNER, CBE, AFC

Royal Air Force
Seletar
c/o GPO Singapore

Ref. SEL/CO/PF/1

Singapore Tel: 84321
Ext 7401

Mrs M R Sugden
20 Edgware Road
RAF Seletar

15 December 1970

Dear Mrs. Sugden,

    I cannot let you depart from Seletar without a personal note of appreciation and thanks for the major contribution you have made during your tour here by your work with the Guides and Brownies, in the Theatre Club, and in many other fields. You gave unsparingly of your own time and devoted a great deal of effort to this wide range of activities, all of which were greatly appreciated by servicemen and civilians alike. As Station Commander I am well aware how important such voluntary contributions are to the life of the station and I am immensely grateful to you for all you have done.

    I wish you and your family a safe journey home and the very best of fortune at Halton.

With kindest regards,

Yours sincerely,

Alec Maisner

By now, and despite 'that incident', my self confidence had improved enormously and I had utilised and developed skills and abilities which I'd had no idea that I possessed.

Singapore 1968

In addition I was leaving with a case full of presents and letters of thanks. And so, with these thoughts to sustain me, we left Singapore,

Once again we were returning to the UK

One Life

Chapter Twenty
RAF Halton: The Last Posting

It was December 1970 and we arrived back in Stratford to be greeted by a thick carpet of snow. Fortunately a bag of coal had been delivered for us and our new neighbours came round to see if we needed anything. We lit a fire and huddled close to get warm whilst airing the bedding and putting a meal together. Then, shivering, and tired-out from our very long journey, we went to bed.

Next morning we walked to find the local shops. Peter had a couple of week's leave before reporting for duty at RAF Halton in Buckinghamshire. This would be our last posting before he retired on reaching the age of forty, and after serving twenty-two years. In these circumstances servicemen were, if possible, given a home posting which would enable them to look for a new permanent home for their family and apply for a job. The rest of us were to remain in Stratford until a married quarter became available. There was a long waiting list.

I could not have wished for a better part of the English countryside for this temporary stay. To add to my happiness the boys came home for the Christmas break and we all enjoyed a good family celebration before they returned to school in January and Peter started his new posting.

I enjoyed living in Stratford. We took full advantage of the historical sites and the time and space helped me to reflect and adjust to the change in pace before another move and upheaval. Then our packing cases arrived from Singapore. Needless to say,

One Life

no sooner had I unpacked them all than we were offered a married quarter! So, once again, I had to pack up and march out.

Our new married quarter was offered with profuse apologies as it had been left filthy by the previous tenants. However, we would be given new furniture and equipment and money to help clean it up. We could have waited longer for a different quarter, but, as always after a parting from Peter, getting together and settling the children in school was my priority. Had I realised just what a task it would be I would probably have waited!

The past tenants would have to pay dearly and they'd be way down the list for a quarter in the future. We soon had the scrubbing and cleaning sorted and stayed for less than a year before being given an ex-officer's quarter nearer to the camp. This one had central heating and a garage. Sheer luxury!

Whilst at RAF Halton we made friends with a dentist and he asked me to work for him on a part time basis. With my nursing qualifications I would be useful when he had patients from the nearby Stoke Mandeville Hospital, especially when the treatment involved an anaesthetist and a nurse to help with chair side and recovery. I readily agreed. He also made visits to carry out dental treatment for MP's and even actors appearing at the theatre in Stratford. I received an extra payment of five pounds, for each of these visits, which was a good deal of money in those days.

Later I was to ask him if he would pay for my exams in dental training to which he replied, 'No, you have the sort of mind that needs new challenges after succeeding in this present one.' He knew me too well.

My health suffered a setback as I had ignored the signs of returning anaemia. One evening I passed out on returning home from a Guide meeting and had to be admitted to hospital. I then had a major operation, a full hysterectomy, followed by three

RAF Halton: The Last Posting

months convalescence before I was able to resume my work. Nevertheless, I was now healthier than I had ever been and I never looked back. My migraines were to recede completely not long after the operation and I had no more seizures. I became fit and healthy.

I resumed my work with the dentist and in the Guiding movement. I'd also joined the Halton Players on moving into the quarter on the RAF base and, in 1972, produced a play for the RAF Training Command Drama Festival. The play, in which Peter acted, was called *The Poker Session*. Although I didn't win this time, I received a fairly good adjudication.

It was now time to make plans for our new life outside of the services and, in particular, what to do about the boy's schooling. Boarding school had proved to be very successful for them both but we would not be able to afford the fees as the grants would dry up on Peter's retirement.

We arranged for an interview for both boys at the well respected Aylesbury Grammar School. Their present headmaster, who understood their situation having had several other service children through his school, forwarded their records and references. After an interview, both boys were accepted to start at Aylesbury Grammar School in the new term.

My expectations for my children, I am sure, were, at times, hard to live with. I loved my children very much. However, my belief in education and moral convictions developed in my own childhood I am sure had some effects on my own children's development.

Andrew went on to gain a total of fifteen GCEs before moving to yet another school, the Grammar School in Bradford, a couple of years later. He was to do well despite the moves, later gaining a degree in graphic design at Liverpool and eventually becoming

One Life

a senior lecturer in digital animation at Edge Hill University.

However, Paul decided he did not want go to another school. He did not want the upheaval and I respected this. He had good GCE results, his progress in the sixth form had been good, and I knew he would not settle into another school. Unhappiness at having to leave his friends, he felt, would get in the way of any progress.

Although in later years Paul may have disagreed with my letting him make this decision at such a young age, he was to go on to achieve great success in his career. He first became an Associate of the Chartered institute of Bankers, then went on to qualify as a barrister-at-law and, after settling in the Channel Islands in 1992, became an Advocate of the Royal Court of Jersey. He is now a partner in a law firm where he specialises in financial regulation. I think we agree now that his decision to leave school early did him no harm after all.

I was really excited at settling down and possibly starting a career myself at last. I'd done nothing but move around from place to place ever since I was fifteen years old. However, I did not realise at the time just how traumatic this was going to be for Peter, who had been looked after in the RAF since joining at the age of eighteen.

His HQ job enabled Peter to plan and look for a job in civilian life and he attended lectures where he was given helpful re-settlement information. This was often a very difficult time for a service man, especially one like Peter who had spent twenty-two years or more being looked after in every aspect of his life. It is only now, on looking back, that I fully appreciate the difficulties, particularly as was the case with those ex-servicemen who stayed near to RAF camps, trying to hang on to the remnants of the old life.

RAF Halton: The Last Posting

Peter did not want to leave the service at all and found the process very unsettling until he was successful in his application for a job working for Bradford Council, his home town. He was to start in this job within a couple of weeks of leaving his service life.

I recognise now that society's expectations, particularly then, that the man in the family would be the breadwinner and hold sole responsibility for the housing and security of his growing family, put a good deal of stress on men leaving the services. For me, on the other hand, there'd been the excitement of new places to see, and the enjoyment of the many benefits of my life shared with Peter.

The local councils, at that time, gave all servicemen from their home town the opportunity to go onto the housing list, and so we had applied for a house some time in advance. When a serviceman's name reached the top of the list, it would be held there until he left the services, so there was a certain amount of security. Peter would receive a pension, and part of this could be commuted to be used as a deposit to buy a house. And, since getting a mortgage was very difficult, the council also had an arrangement whereby certain building societies would give priority to an ex-serviceman's application.

Unlike Peter, I was delighted and excited to be starting a new life. I'd have my own home to do what I wanted with: my own choice in decorations, and at long last I'd be settled in one place. Living in Yorkshire did not pose a problem for me either. After all, I had no ties with my relatives and had been away from London since I was seventeen – nearly twenty-three years.

We decided that I would move into a council house in Bradford, as soon as possible, and settle Andrew and Jeanine into their new school in time for the start of term. Paul, who was now settled in his job at the bank, would stay on with his Dad and

One Life

Darren, who would continue going to nursery school. I could then look for a temporary job to help pay to furnish the house for six.

Looking back, now thirty-something years on, I can see I threw myself into this new life with my usual naive enthusiasm. My health was restored and I was blessed with four wonderful children who I felt sure would all grow into confident and capable adults. Peter and I had done our best for them. I began to realise that I had created my own family, the one I'd never had. Like all families, it had its own trials and tribulations, but we'd learned to deal with them, and we were all, by and large, happy people. I wasn't too worried about Peter settling in Civvy Street: he'd dealt with tough times before.

I wasn't thinking too far ahead; why should I have? I was coming up to forty years old; I'd marched out of RAF quarters for the last time. From now on, I'd be marching on, determined to live life to the full. I might have thought I had come to the end of a life of adventures, dramas, and sadness and that I was just there for much happiness. I had no grand plan. I knew eventually my children would, one by one, fly the nest. Until then, I would be there, come what may, determined to do my best, and enjoying it.